Instinctive Fly Fishing

Instinctive Fly Fishing

A Guide's Guide to Better Trout Fishing

Revised and Expanded

Second Edition

Taylor Streit

Illustrations by Pete Chadwell

LYONS PRESS

Guilford, Connecticut

An imprint of Globe Pequot Press

For Chelsea, Mom, and Blanca

To buy books in quantity for corporate use
or incentives, call **(800) 962–0973**
or e-mail **premiums@GlobePequot.com**.

Lyons Press is an imprint of Globe Pequot Press.

Text design and layout artist: Sue Murray

Photos by Taylor Streit unless otherwise noted
Illustrations by Pete Chadwell

Library of Congress Cataloging-in-Publication Data is available on file.

ISBN 978-0-7627-7362-6

Printed in United States of America

10 9 8 7 6 5 4 3 2

Contents

Acknowledgments

On looking back over a lifetime of fly fishing, I realize that many fine fishermen and writers helped make this book. The first of these was, quite appropriately, my dad, the late Phil Streit, who plopped me onto the bank of a stream in New York fifty years ago. Then, when I was a kid on foot, Mike Lucas, Bill Luty, Herb Dickerson, and Pat Keating all found time to take me fishing. Special thanks to the late Fran Betters for officially getting me started in the fly-fishing business in my teens.

After moving to New Mexico I was tutored by Bill Vickers, Charlie Reynolds, and Mike Wiley. In later years I have learned a lot from New Mexicans Chris Jarvis, Justin Spence, Garrett VeneKlasen, Keith Loveless, and Bob Widgren.

Heavy Rolle and Felix Smith of South Andros, Bahamas, taught me tricks with their "trow lines." Argentines Lorenzo Sympson and Pedro Arencet have added to my education.

My great crew of guides is always finding new ways to outwit trout, and much of the new work in this edition has come from their contributions. So many thanks to Brian Spilman, Christoph Engle, Daniel Gentle, and Derek Gordon.

And I have learned a lot from many outstanding fishermen whom I have guided—too many to name, but Dale White Sr. and Shane Mills come to mind.

And many thanks to that famous Colorado angler, my brother Jackson Streit, who has contributed much to this book.

Many fine writers have helped me along with this project, including Tracy McCallum, Nick Lyons, John Nichols, Tom Taylor, John Judy, Jack Handey, Dan Boyne, Richard Atkinson, Bill Luty, Greg Belcamino, and Pete Susca.

Last but not least is my son Nick, who helped immensely with many aspects of this book. I may have taught him to fish, but he has gone way past what I gave him to become an incredible guide in his own right.

The late Fran Betters, the Ausable Wulff.

Introduction

Long before I was a fishing guide I was a fly fisherman. Much of what I knew about the sport—or thought I knew—came from reading and learning from other fly fishers. When the "sport" turned into a profession, I discovered that there is a big difference between being a casual fisherman and having to feed your family by fishing. Most of my faintly conceived notions couldn't stand up against the naked truth of experience. Now, after thirty years of guiding, my perceptions about catching trout are based on personal experience.

Being a "commercial fisherman" has shown me that the keys to fly-fishing success are usually just commonsense rules of nature: keep the sun at your back and your fly in the water; think like a predator. Such observations are rather mundane details, and that makes them unpopular with complicated fly-fishing types. We fly fishers revel in complexity and choose convoluted solutions over simple ones.

This has a lot to do with our times. When I started fly fishing, folks were more connected with the natural world than they are now. It was a more rural land then, and people spent more time outdoors. Many were already hunters and fishermen, and taking up fly fishing was just part of a natural progression that started with bait fishing and went on to spinners before graduating to the fly rod. They learned a lot about trout and the ways of Mother Nature along the way.

In the new millennium most of us are strangers in the natural world. With everything computerized, categorized, and virtualized, the modern fly fisher has developed an overly technical and analytical approach to the sport. His leaders need to be constructed with micrometers; the thorax of his fly needs to be tied out of opossum— not common 'possum, mind you, but the rare Siberian opossum. Overburdened with all these theories, formulas, and flies, he splashes ungracefully into the stream. Dragging all those ideas along can be more of a burden than an asset. Knowledge and gear don't, in themselves, make a fisherman, and they are poor substitutes for simply knowing how to fish.

The author with a monster brown trout. Instincts and common sense play big roles in becoming a good fisherman.

But defining "how to fish" is elusive. You can't see it, taste it, or smell it, but we all know that some people know how to fish a heck of a lot better than others. The problem is that many of the things that make a great fisherman are things that he does instinctively and sub-consciously. Ask him why he ducked there or chose to fish a pool from that particular spot, and he wouldn't know.

A few years ago I tried to get this down on paper. I sat and typed at the computer, but what came out sounded too much like most of what I had been reading all my life. I finally realized that much of what I was trying to capture was intuitive, predatory skills too slippery to be so easily caught and written down. I concluded that the only place to get in touch with this primal fisherman is on the water. So, over a period of several years I yapped into a little tape recorder. I kept notes on both stream and lake, in New Mexico, Colorado, and Argentina, with clients who represented every phase of the learning curve.

The tapes revealed that the modern fly fisher's instincts are indeed hidden deep in the forest—on the back branches of his family tree—and that on the trout stream common sense "ain't common." In between all the screwups and blunders, tangled lines and hooked thumbs, a lot of trout were caught, however, and I paid careful attention to the often-subtle reasons why those fish took the fly. I found that a thousand factors helped catch them, many of which I had never noticed in all my years of guiding. What follows are those thousand—and one—things.

MORE INSTINCTIVE FLY FISHING

Although I was happy with my original *Instinctive Fly Fishing,* there have been many occasions while out fishing when a pearl of fly-fishing wisdom rises, and I think, "Damn it, I should have put that in the book!" So I started to jot down notes for *Instinctive Fly Fishing* and have now realized that the first book just scratched the surface in many aspects.

There are new tips, knots, and specifics on common hatches. There are observations on fishing and casts that we have been using for years but never really analyzed until now—like the Cimarron sling and the lift-and-snap. And in what seems an overlooked subject, there is a travel section, where I try to put anglers in good water on their next fishing trip.

I have come to realize that much of the premise of the original book was based on the idea that if you find the fish difficult to catch, just go to the lengths necessary to find dumber ones. This is an elitist stance perhaps because many of us have to fish with crowds on public water—on Saturday afternoons, no less. So this edition deals more with catching overly smart trout and their dysfunctional cousins, the slow-witted—but neurotic—stockers.

1

Instinctive Fly Fishing

"If industrial man continues to multiply his numbers and expand his operations he will succeed in his apparent intention, to seal himself off from the natural and isolate himself within a synthetic prison of his own making."

—Edward Abbey, *Desert Solitaire*

The osprey dangles above the water on beating wings—intense eyes fixed on its prey. Every atom in its body has but one goal: catch the fish. It doesn't chat with itself while this is going on: "Perhaps I should go around the next bend; this trout is too deep." The animal instinctively knows the answer. A decision is made from somewhere deep inside. The fluttering wings become rigid, and the bird whirls and plunges. When the water explodes above the trout, the startled creature has but a wisp of time to flee. The fish that ponders will be eaten.

The human fisherman doesn't have—or have to have—a fraction of that concentration. He's just standing there in midstream, mouth ajar, staring into his fly box. At times he may actually be fishing, but he's as likely to be puttering around the edges of it rather than actually doing it. "Should I try that pool up there?" he asks himself. "Maybe with a different fly? Didn't I read that—oh, was that a splash? Did I just have a strike? Where was I?"

Few of us ever get to the gifted state that is all action, and if and when we do reach that blissful place where instincts guide movements, it usually can be captured only fleetingly. Michael Jordan's "zone," the music in Mozart's ear—that God-given state of genius is unobtainable to those who are constantly supposing, thinking, and changing flies.

The instinctive fly fisherman may not stand out in a crowd—but you'll know one when you see one. *Peter Lloyd*

Certainly the intellectual will sink a basket here and there, but the real pro knows that when it is time to play, instincts rule the game.

It is on rare occasions that you will spot this instinctive fisherman on the water. He doesn't stand out, and your eyes would more likely be drawn to the person midstream winging a long line. To the untrained eye the long caster is the one who looks the part, whereas the real expert may not attract much attention. He's slinking along the bank, dangling a few feet of line in carefully chosen spots. His movements are those of an animal on the prowl rather than of an urban technician. He isn't hampered with the second guesses that shame most anglers out of the action. It isn't a bubbly "top of the morning to you" attitude, just a confidence that says, "A fish is going to eat my fly any second!" This guy may have little faith in life, other people, and himself. Maybe that is why this loner fishes so much. His positivity makes him all eyes, all ears, all present and accounted for.

Another phenomenon that I have observed is called, for lack of a better word, luck. Yes, that's what we call it, but that isn't exactly what it is. Put two guys of seemingly equal talent on the water, and one will almost always outfish the other. I see this all the time when guiding: The one whom you assume will catch a lot of fish doesn't. This fellow often talks a good game but may have no feel for the outdoors. His ability to not catch fish is astounding, and he does the wrong thing at just the right time. He will take the fly out of the water just as a trout is rising to eat it. I'll jump a foot into the air and say, "Didn't you see that fish?"

"No," he will say. The guy wades up a stream like a grizzly chasing salmon, and when he finally hooks a fish he fights it with a delicacy equal to that of the bear.

The other guy, the one who catches trout, has a commonsense nature that is responsive to instructions from the guide, the stream, and the fish. He may not even know many of the details of the sport, but they are the easy part. They can be learned.

Although no easy matter, the instinctive, the intuitive, can be learned, and you can become "lucky," too. I have guided many people who were at first out of place on the water, but I've found that if they stick with it, they start fitting in and eventually become good, natural fly fishers.

How does the modern fly fisherman get schooling in Mother Nature's ways? First, you must eliminate that which interferes with your focused pursuit of fish. This may mean as little as tidying up your fishing vest or as much as tidying up your way of life. Maybe it's your stressful job, cranky spouse, or boisterous kids who are keeping you distracted and out of the water. If any of these factors get in the way of your fly fishing, they gotta go! I know that some of you will hem and haw on this, so for those who are not willing to go to such lengths, here are some watered-down suggestions—compromises, if you will— that should help bring more cohesion between human and fish.

Do things that get you in touch with your natural self: meditate, smell flowers, get off that choppy hip-hop and listen to something that flows, like Vivaldi or Coltrane. And go fishing, of course. I don't mean fly fishing. Get yourself a cane pole, some stink bait, and a bobber and head to the catfish hole. Don't scoff at the idea of bait fishing; there's

Why do fish like this start biting at certain times? Why do they stop? Truly observant anglers often know.

a lot to be learned from it. Bait fishing offers one thing that fly fishing lacks—foreplay. There's a heavenly period when you are letting the fish eat your worm, which doesn't happen when fishing with most artificials. The rod is tapping, the line is tugging, and you become filled with anticipation because you know the throbbing rod comes next!

When your catfish is safely ashore, whack it on the head and then yank the skin off with pliers. If you get your hands covered with guts and stuck by catfish spikes, so much the better. While lounging on the bank after you have barbecued your fish be sure to watch the wind shake the leaves on the trees and notice how the clouds grow and drift. Take your shoes off, stand in the mud, and let it ooze up between your toes. Whatever you do, don't—I repeat, don't—take along any reading about the life cycle of aquatic insects. Suggested reading could include "Big Two-Hearted River" by Hemingway or the works of Roderick Haig-Brown.

Haig-Brown writes with the skill and simplicity of someone who has mastered his craft. He spent his life outdoors and sees beyond the frivolous details to the basic elements: water and weather conditions, amount of fishing pressure, timing, and attitude. In *A River Never*

Sleeps, he writes about difficult fish: ". . . they always like it; they aren't chalk-stream fish or even fish that live near a city; they'll come if it looks like food." He made that comment when faced with a fish that wouldn't take the fly that he always used at that place and circumstance. He ultimately did have to change flies and tactics to catch it, but he wisely started out with the premise that the animals are dumb. That way he could just go along catching them with a tried-and-true method and fly until he ran into a smart fish. He didn't get to the water and invent problems and complications; he simply fished and dealt with a situation when it arose.

He writes that he didn't catch any large fish on a particular day because the water was warm. End of story. He didn't wrack his brain about this. It is simply a fact that larger trout don't feed well in warm water. All the fly changing in the world won't alter that. Certain things may work better than others under those circumstances, but if the angler remembers the elementary fact about water temperature, he will make better decisions about where and how to fish.

And fish just don't eat all the time. All species of fish are subject to this rule, and all species of fishermen, especially fly fishermen, are reluctant to accept this rule. When faced with the dilemma, a fly fisherman will change flies and fish harder rather than take a nap or watch the river flow—something to get him rested so that when the fish do start feeding, the angler will be fresh and ready. You'll probably learn a lot more by watching from your observation post than you would by beating the water to a froth. Like why and when the fish start biting. Usually there is a subtle change of weather that turns on the fish—or insects.

Maybe you could plan your next trip away from the popular tailwaters. Shoulder-to-shoulder fishing for big trout brings out the worst in many anglers. I find myself cramming my lunch down my throat while cursing at the guy across the river who has the audacity to catch more fish than I do. Fishing smaller, more-remote streams with spooky little trout will develop your predatory instincts. There you will discover the importance of keeping the sun at your back and of staying low and in the shade. The skills you pick up will be beneficial in all other fishing situations.

Another helpful pursuit that has fallen out of favor in some fly-fishing circles is hunting—taking quiet steps in the shadows, crawling, and slipping between trees. It demands all of one's senses and intelligence. When fresh sign is spotted, instincts as old as time arise, the nostrils open, ears and eyes strain, and the clutter in the mind clears. The human animal is again in his natural place.

And most helpful is being observant on the water. You'll absorb a lot more information than you might realize that will later spill out as intuition. Someday you'll be able to just stick your head out the door and sense if the fish are biting: Your nose will catch the scent of the still, moist air that trout love; your eyes will notice that the light is slanted about right; and before you know it, you'll be on your way to the river wondering how the fly rod found its way into your hand.

2

Fly-Fishing Personalities

Spending the day with folks engaged in the intense game of fly fishing will teach you a lot about people. After years of observing my fellow fishermen I now feel qualified as an amateur psychologist and ready to pontificate on the subject of fly-fishing personalities. Following are several that I have identified.

The author and his son Nick, also an established fishing guide and owner of Taos Fly Shop. Between them, they have seen all types of fishermen.

ANALYTICAL FLY FISHERMAN

The analytical fly fisherman keeps so busy fiddling with his formulas, strategies, and entomological charts that the simple, straightforward solutions to catching a fish are often overlooked. If, for instance, he can't catch a fish, he should examine the obvious first: Has the fish actually seen the fly? Has the fish seen him? Heck, maybe the fish can't even see. I once approached a client who was casting to a dead trout lying on the bottom of the river. He told me that it wouldn't "take" and was showing the decomposing animal a new fly as I arrived. To first study the condition of such a docile creature might have been the commonsense thing to do, but, as a cabby once told me, "Common sense ain't common."

THE JIGGLER

The jiggler is a stressed-out breed of cat commonly found residing in large cities. Far removed from his ancestral homeland his senses get overloaded when near trout water. And when approaching said water his body vibrates as if it were electrically charged, thereby oscillating the fly rod to form a tangled ball of line, leader, and fly. Although cardiac problems are a possibility, there are more practical concerns: This angler's fly seldom sits still long enough to catch a fish. The jiggler also changes flies often, always thinking that the next choice will be the right one. With those shaky fingers, however, it is a time-consuming process and should be avoided.

If the jiggler should somehow hook a good fish, the chances are slim that it will be landed. If a person is that excitable before a trout is actually hooked, imagine what happens when he latches onto one. The hyper angler hates to give a fish line and can generally be counted on to freeze hysterically when a big fish takes, breaking the leader and losing the treasure.

The jiggler will invariably generate unnecessary tension in the casting arm, and that rigidity takes the feel out of the casting operation. Because he cannot feel the line loading, the timing of the cast becomes a guessing game. His uncertainty tends to make him perform many needless false casts.

THE SLACKER

The lazy angler doesn't take care of his slack line. When I'm guiding I usually say a hundred times a day, "Pick up the slack, please—all of it." Most anglers are guilty of this serious infraction. These are often the same fishermen who do not extend their arm far enough when reaching. And very few "slackers" wade close enough to their targets. When compiled, these details add up to bad drifts and missed strikes.

These items are dealt with later in the book but are of such significance that—just like I do with my guiding clients—I will start nagging you now so you will get your money's worth by the end of the book.

I remember a client who complained about the day's fishing. He didn't have any right to because he fished with one hand in his pocket all day! With all the slack lying about, he spent his time tangled with rocks, brush, and his appendages. His fly was out of the water—and the fish's mouth as well.

Fishing in streams, if done correctly, is a lot of work. Try that difficult cast under the brush, or see what's up that channel you've never fished. Save lazy for the catfish hole.

Another kind of lazy angler is epitomized by an old friend, Billy, who has a house on the Batten Kill. The river is known for its fabulous Trico hatch, but the tiny black and white mayfly does its elaborate metamorphosis in the mornings only—providing some of the most interesting and inspired feeding in a trout's world. But when I asked Billy how he does in the hatch, he said that he "doesn't fish in the mornings." He is an excellent fisherman and drives for hours to get to this house on the river and worked for fifty years in the corporate world to get it. So we know he is not lazy. He buys all the right gear and ties great flies, but by this omission in his fishing repertoire he gets graded as a "casual" fisherman. Sorry, Bill.

Staying late is another important factor that separates the pros from the amateurs. Few fishers—including me—fish as late as we should in summer, which is until *dark*. In warm weather, larger brown trout come out *only* then. If you are doing it right you should be using your flashlight to find the car.

THE FLY-FISHING SNOB

We fly fishers have a deeply ingrained sense of superiority that sometimes gives us a bad name. (Well, a bad name to bait fishermen anyway.) The real fly-fishing upper crust is wrapped up in the mystique of the sport and develops particular ideas about what's right and wrong. Perhaps fishing only dries made from natural materials and delivering them with a wisp of a bamboo rod. Heaven knows how people come to profound opinions over such a trivial pursuit as ours. I think the Brits are responsible: For instance, you can't fish with weight or strike indicators in the U.K., but you can thump all the trout you catch. (But only with a "proper" tool; a priest it's called—for God's sake.)

With the U.K. leading the way and the United States close behind, there seems to be some correlation between this level of snobbery and the closer to doom your civilization has advanced.

THE TROUT BUM

There are about half a million young trout bums in the United States. I admit that I was such a pest myself, although a funkier version thereof. This new breed of trout bum drives a Toyota 4Runner, spends a lot of time on the water, and with all that youthful energy catches all our damn trout. And if you have one of these varmints living in your neighborhood, encourage him to get a family and job so that the nearby fish will be released unharmed.

THE OVERQUALIFIED FLY FISHER

Certain fly fishers know too much for their own good. We guide them on our small streams here in New Mexico, and they are forever casting too far, mending too much, and thinking too often.

It is common for this type of angler to be accompanied by a beginner (see "Bluegills and Bobbers," Chapter 15) and be thoroughly outfished by the beginner. The beginner has the loose mind and short cast that are more effective on a lot of water.

THE OVEREAGER ANGLER

The overeager angler gets so obsessed that he pounds the water like a lunatic. When you find yourself doing this, listen to the little gurgling noises, take deep breaths, and remember that it's only fishing. Thinking there just might be a nice fish behind every rock, this person tends to fish every inch of stream in sight. All really good fishermen have a no-doubt outlook, believing that each cast is going to catch a fish, but that attitude needs to be tempered with good judgment, or else there will be a lot of wasted effort.

Such overeager anglers start pulling line out for the next cast while they are fishing the present one (thinking it is necessary to always make a longer cast). This is sloppy and distracts from fishing the cast that is on the water. If you are a good hand with the rod, you may be able to pull line out of the reel at the same time as you are fishing. But no matter how much experience you have, you'll catch more fish if you do one thing at a time.

FIRED-UP FLY FISHER

The fired-up fly fisher is so dedicated that he gets worn out before the dance starts. No matter what your mind says, the body has only so much juice in it, so plan your time wisely. For instance, the long evenings of early summer can provide the best hatches and fishing of the season, so I often try to convince wound-up clients that we shouldn't start early in the morning. Not wanting to appear to be a slacker, however, I seldom push it. Invariably these people tire and want to quit around sundown, just when things start to happen. Or they will be so pooped by then that they end up doing a sloppy job and missing all the strikes.

THE MATERIALISTIC FISHERMAN

We all like to catch big fish, but for many that's the only criterion used to judge the quality of the day. Materialistic fishermen are so focused on achieving their goal that they seldom get to receive the full benefits a day outside can provide. All they care about are results—and that means big fish, period! A couple of years ago I was guiding a guy on the Chama River here in New Mexico, and the fishing was so good that I couldn't get my angler to look at the bird overhead—an albino red-tailed hawk. The startling bird sailed this way and that and then perched on a tree branch. I was giving my client updates on the movement of this once-in-a-lifetime sight, but he never raised his head to look. We fished up around the bend, and he didn't see it. Such guys (you guessed it: the materialistic fisher is most always male) are usually myopic anglers who would actually catch more trout if they became more aware of the world around them.

THE DRIFTER

Another common and amusing sort of fly fisher is the drifter. You can take him from town to country, but his mind seldom accompanies him.

Bob is a good case in point. I was having a heck of a time trying to teach Chicago Bob to cast. Bob was one of those laugh-a-minute cats who is always looking for a joke—even if it is at his expense—so I'm sure that he wouldn't mind me telling you this little tale. (He may have even planned the whole thing.)

We were in the middle of a stream where I was trying to teach Bob to cast and fish. He seemed to have finally gotten somewhat of a loose grip on the casting operation, so I went off to check on his partner. I returned a short while later to see if he had had any luck. As I walked across a meadow I could see Bob in the distance making some puzzling motions with his fly rod. Bob's casting had deteriorated beyond my expectations, which were not high. His line was traveling in wide, circular loops, and his arm had to go around and around like a windmill to maintain a sort of lasso effect. Getting closer, I was able to analyze the problem and called out.

"Hey, Bob, there is a fish on your line." When I reached Bob he told me that he had been having difficulty with his casting for some time. The very dead look of the 4-inch trout supported the idea that the fish had been attached for some time.

THE OPEN-MINDED ANGLER

The open-minded angler uses the experience and expertise acquired on his home water elsewhere but is not a slave to it. All trout streams are different, and if you step into new water with a lot of preconceived notions, you may go fishless. A good example of this occurs when a tailwater fisherman fishes a new trout stream. Because he is used to being surrounded by both fish and fishermen, he is programmed to move at a slow pace. This is inappropriate for a normal trout stream because a regular freestone stream doesn't hold as many fish as a tailwater stream. The trout, less pressured in the freestone stream, might take a fly the first time it goes over their head. Consequently, covering lightly fished water quickly is wise.

Are you an open-minded fisherman? Lazy? Overeager? Personality makes a difference when fishing.

This open-minded angler pays attention to what is going on around him and goes at a relaxed enough pace that he can absorb the subtle hints that nature constantly supplies to the observant. This person also solicits help and advice from others and is willing to learn new things.

In general, however, fishermen have sensitive egos, so, as with the rest of the human race, open-mindedness and self-analysis are not common. Who ever heard an angler blame himself for a poor day's fishing? "I was off my game." No, quotes like that are for sports that don't have so many built-in excuses. Fishermen have been graciously excluded from personal responsibility ever since the first one of our kind stooped through the cave door with an empty stringer and grunted, "They aren't biting." We fly fishers are above such common lies and have developed a plethora of elaborate excuses appropriate to our lofty position in the hierarchy of fishing. "I didn't have any No. 26s," "My leader wasn't fluorocarbon," and "My guide sucked" are just a few.

Do you identify with any of these personality disorders? Rehabilitation is possible if you are ready to put the responsibility where it belongs—on yourself. If we do that, we will become better fishermen—and people.

3

Tips

Here is a potpourri of tips I have gathered from my fly-fishing and guiding experience. Hopefully, they can help you catch more fish and increase the enjoyment of the outing.

USE WIDE-GAP HOOKS

I have kept score on the hookup percentages and found that flies tied on hooks with narrow gaps do not hook and hold fish. Flies tied on them should be sold for scrap. Wide-gap hooks catch more fish!

KEEP HOOKS SHARP

If you miss several fish, check your fly's sharpness by running the hook point against your fingernail at a steep angle. If it digs in, it's sharp; if it slides, it needs sharpening. If you don't have a hook sharpener, pick up one of those smooth river rocks at your feet and hone the point with it.

WALKING PAYS OFF

We do a lot of walking in Argentina and the southern Rockies where I fish and guide. I prefer to fish water that hasn't been hammered, and, for my money, with each mile walked and each hill climbed, the quality of both the fishing and the experience rises dramatically. Get the walking over with at the beginning of the day if possible. This usually means hiking downriver and then fishing back up. Try to time the hike so that when you start fishing the fish will have just started biting (usually in the late morning, depending on weather and hatches). Don't rig the rod until the planned destination is reached. Then it won't get stuck in the brush all the time. Besides, putting casts here and there as you go is a half-assed way to fish, and you will more likely spook more than you'll catch. Instead, scout as you walk and look for insects and indications

Sharp hooks make a difference on tough-jawed old fish like this.

that will clue you in on how and what to fish. When ready to choose a fly and style of fishing, listen to your instincts. They may have learned more on the walk than you consciously realized.

POINT YOUR ROD FORWARD

When strolling, crawling, and swearing your way through brush, keep your rod pointed in front of you. This gives you more control, allowing you to aim it where you would like. And if you do get it stuck, you don't have to go back to where you've already been to set the fly free. When going through willows, raise your arm and point the rod straight up.

Another argument for pointing the rod forward is that the tip section of a three- or four-piece rod may get pulled off on a bush behind you. And you won't notice this until you arrive at water's edge, and the tip section is a way back yonder someplace. Having the rod strung up in some fashion will prevent losing a section.

EASY WAY TO THREAD YOUR LINE AND LEADER

Rather than trying to finagle an invisible and slippery leader end through the guides, fold the fly line over double and run it through the guides. It

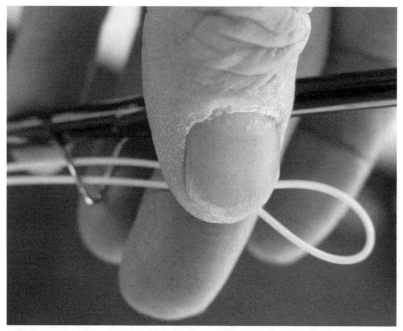

Fold the fly line into a loop when stringing up the rod. *Wes Edling*

is more manageable, and if it escapes your fingers, it won't scamper back down the rod like a leader end will. When fishing close, use a leader of just 5 to 7 feet.

GO WITH THE FLOW

Don't get frustrated by trying to catch your fly in the wind. Point the rod into the blow and let it come to you.

FORGET SOMETHING?

Ever find that you have forgotten something when you reach the stream? Of course, you have. Then try the "patdown." Start by patting your head: "Yes, I have a hat on." Continue down the body by checking for the appropriate gear for that section, finishing the body count with, "Yes, I have my shoes on." Close your eyes and make a pretend cast, then mentally picture all the gear you need for that: flies, leaders, rod, reel, line, and anything else. Ask yourself what you need should you hook a fish and so on.

When you set off from the car to fish, stash the keys under a rock near the car and tell your fishing companion where the rock is. Doing this will minimize the chance of losing the keys in the river and allow said fishing mate to get into the auto. Also use a length of baling wire to attach an extra key somewhere under the car. Those magnetic key containers come off when you drive over brush.

KEEP YOUR FLY CLEAN

Fish will seldom eat a fly when it has *any* foreign material on it. The fly should be checked *often*—especially when you are fishing in mossy streams.

Cleaning debris from flies can be time-consuming, but you usually won't have to manually remove moss from a fly if you learn this little trick. Make a very short and wicked cast that snaps the fly right at the surface. When you make the cast, think of cracking a whip, so that the end of the whip—your fly—hits the water at the speed of sound. If done properly, this type of cast will clean the moss off the fly most of the time. If you are fishing with a lot of weight and have to sling the fly around in an oval, modify the slap. Just as the fly meets the surface, rip it back as fast as you can. Of course, cast away from where you are fishing so as not to alert the quarry.

DURABLE FLIES

Tired of flies falling apart? Here is a tip I learned from international angler Garrett VeneKlasen while fishing with him for peacock bass in the Amazon. Tie your flies with superglue instead of head cement. If you don't tie the flies you fish, put a tiny drop behind the heads of those you use. Then, contrary to the desires of the fly manufacturers, they will last forever.

FLY BOXES

Serious anglers stay up late into the long winter's night organizing their flies for the fishing season ahead. They might have one box for small mayflies, one for nymphs, and another one for who knows what. When they get to the water months later for the "goober" hatch, they have things planned just so and grab the goober box. But when they get a mile from the truck they find that the trout are eating pink goobers and that they have brought only the box of red stripped goobers. The unexpected is the norm in nature, so have one fly box that contains every kind of goober fly you can think of.

If you've never lost one of these dear boxes of flies, you haven't fished enough. My client Mark Yarbrough puts his name and phone number on all his fly boxes and then waterproofs his labeling with a covering of transparent tape. (Offering a reward for their return is another option.)

KEEP YOUR SOCKS CLEAN

To avoid getting your socks covered with earthen materials when changing in and out of your waders, keep a little piece of carpet (or floor mat from the vehicle) to stand on when you change in and out of your gear.

CARS AND RODS

I have had fly rods broken by all sorts of critters, but the nastiest varmint is the automobile, so minimize exposure to it when possible. And when gearing up, take your rod out of the vehicle last. Reverse the order at the end of the day, putting the rod away first. Never lean rods in the convenient wedge made by an open door. Leaning a rod against the side of the car is a bad idea, too, because it has no purchase and can slide. (Although magnetic gadgets are sold to secure them.) If you must have a rigged rod near the auto, lean it against trees a few feet away from the action. Don't forget that it's there. Finally, when you're finished for the day, don't put your rod on top of your car. It is easy to drive off and forget it, as I've done—twice!

If you do break your rod, don't let it end the day. I once caught three 19-inchers with just the butt section of a rod. It wasn't pretty, but it was three 19-inchers better than going to the house.

DRY-FLY RESUSCITATION

When your hackled dry flies get crushed and matted, you can restore them with steam. Hold the fly with forceps or pliers over the steam vented from a boiling teakettle, and watch the hackles spring to life before your very eyes!

EYEWEAR

Every fisherman should always wear polarized sunglasses for seeing the fish and the bottom. This makes for safer wading and increased eye comfort. (Also a hook in the eye is the most common serious fishing injury.) Tan is the best all-around shade and reduces glare under faint light. If you wear prescription eyeglasses, try either clip-ons or—better yet—"fit-over" polarized sunglasses. Don't forget to take your regular glasses along if you are going to fish into the evening. Magnifiers can be helpful in tying flies on, and some attach to the brim of your hat.

LEAVE YOUR WHITE HAT AT HOME

Always wear some sort of brimmed hat to see better and help protect your eyes.

Avoid white hats when fishing over spooky fish. White stands out more than any other color.

REEL HANDY ADVICE

I recommend setting up the reel so that you wind with your primary hand. You do have to switch hands to get a fish on the reel, but you get used to that, and you can reel much more adeptly with your primary hand. This is important when you are fighting a fish that swims at you because hooks often fall out when tension is lost. Trout don't usually swim very fast, but when a bonefish charges you, you have to reel very fast in order to take up the slack. This setup also frees your primary hand to actually land the fish.

TANGLES AND SNAGS

A big factor in catching fish is having the bait in the water as much as possible. Snarls in the line can infringe on that precious time. And unlike the fish's appetite, this is something we have control over and can improve upon. The first rule about tangles is: Don't get frustrated. I know that is easier said than done, but everyone gets tangles. They are just a part of fishing. (Although they can also be a sign of poor casting or lack of attention.) Tangles get compounded when they are recast, so notice how the fly lands on the water; if it comes down funny, take the

Reeling with your primary hand gives you an edge—plus, holding the rod in your other hand frees your number one hand for netting and landing. When fighting big fish, holding the rod in a high position can help to steer the fish.

line in *gently* for inspection. Hopefully you can unravel the tangle early enough so that it doesn't need to be cut and retied.

A tangle isn't really a *knot*, but if you pull on the mess it will soon become a knot, and as a tight knot, it will put a kink in the leader and weaken it. Proceed slowly, and you will start to see how to get out of the mess. There are sit-down and standing tangles. In either case, if you are out in the river, put the rod under your arm and use your mouth as a "third hand" to help unsnarl. Check to see if the nipper tool you have has a pointy thing in it for this. If not, the point of a fly hook also works well for getting in there and pulling loops apart.

First ask yourself if it is so bad that you should just cut it off and start all over again. Sometimes partial amputation is the best solution. If you are fishing a tandem rig, cut off the bottom fly, and it will then unwrap much easier.

WIND KNOTS

Check for wind knots often. Remember that they reduce the strength of your leader by 50 percent and should never be allowed to remain. If detected early, they can be opened with a hook point; even better, use two hook points, one in each hand, and get them into the knot. If you can't open and untie the knot, cut the leader and start over.

Wind knots should actually be called casting knots because they have nothing to do with the wind and everything to do with casting. A casting instructor can show you why you are making them (tailing loops) and how to improve your cast so they won't happen.

OTHER TANGLES

Master guide John Judy of Sisters, Oregon, pointed out to me that when people reel line with the nondominant (left) hand, the rod wobbles, causing tangles around the rod tip. If you reel with your nonprimary hand, reel smoothly, and watch the rod while you reel. If you see it start to tangle, reel more slowly.

If the tangle is at the end of the rod, lower it as gingerly as possible so that nothing gets jostled on the way down.

If you aren't careful, another tangle can form when a loop of line swings around and around the rod. Look along the rod at the tangle before you do anything with it; you may find that you can flip the middle section of the mess back around the rod the way it came.

If a fly gets tangled around the end of the rod, don't jiggle or jostle it because doing that will send the fly around the rod a dozen more times.

When a tangle occurs at the top end of a long fly rod, it is, of course, necessary to get the mess in front of you so that you can straighten it out. If you are on the bank, you can just put the reel down to get at the snarl. If you are in the middle of the river, don't be afraid to put the reel into the water. I see clients going through all sorts of contortions to keep their reel dry. It's only water, and it is actually a good idea to dunk your reel now and then to get the sand out of it. Of course, keep all gear out of salt water, and be sure to keep reels dry that have cork drags—they are thankfully rare anymore.

Another kind of tangle forms in your reel over time if you wind your leader all the way into your reel; the end will worm its way under other coils of line. The next time you pull line out of the reel, this loop will slide down the fly line to eventually lodge in the backing. If you fish a lot, this happens over and over until you can have quite a mess brewing down there. This is easily averted if you just don't reel the line in all the way and leave a few inches of leader sticking out of the reel.

IT'S THE GUIDE'S JOB — WELL, SOMETIMES

I conduct a guides school that meets every spring, and many of the students—well, actually, *all* the students—dream of getting paid to "do what they love." And as part of the reality check, I regret to inform them that dealing with tangles is like the sight of blood to a doctor—you'd better get used to it. Different guides have different policies on undoing clients' tangles, and for my part I seem to have a different policy daily (probably dependent on how much I have been guiding). Some guides justifiably feel like it is part of an angler's training to learn to undo tangles. But we want our fisherman's flies in the water, so we may go ahead and undo the tangle. This is especially the case if the person is giving it a go and getting nowhere.

Which brings me to some advice for older clients on this subject: If you are having trouble getting your trusty guide to unravel your mess, say, "I didn't bring my magnifying glasses." And when you get the tangle in hand, hold the mess out at arm's length and squint a lot. If your guide is snoring in the bushes, stamp your feet, throw your rod onto the ground, and make sighing noises. Unless you have a very compliant sort of guide—a rare cut of guide because we are generally rebellious by nature—the worst way to get your tangles undone is to move your rod so the tangle is right in front of his eyes. When I have a client who does that, he or she gets that one done for free, but it isn't long before I am taking up "strategic positions" to spot fish from and yelling "attaboy" encouragement from yonder hill. (A note for younger guides: "Yonder hill" has to be far enough that the average tangle will be unsnarled by the time you make the walk.)

When you take your assembled fishing rods for a car or boat ride, they might behave well at first, but they'll eventually get tangled in cramped quarters. By the time you reach your destination, they will likely be all enmeshed. My brother Jackson Streit showed me how to keep the rascals under control.

First, for each rod be sure the fly is secured in the keeper or impaled in the cork handle, with the line just barely snug. Next, grasp the line outside the rod about halfway up the rod and wrap it around the rod three times. Finally, take the line that is coming out of the reel and wrap it around the back of the reel. (It is necessary to take a little line out of the reel to do this.) This will keep the line snug against the rod, where it can't get into trouble.

SNAGGED

A few tricks can help prevent you from having to physically unhook a fly snagged on rocks or brush. The benefit of getting unstuck from afar, besides saving you a walk, is that you're less likely to spook the fish between you and the errant fly. (A guide may often carry an extra rod—handy when the fly is snagged near a fish or a particularly promising spot.)

Various snags hold onto flies differently. A fly hooked to a submerged rock will usually let go if it is pulled from the opposite direction from which it was hooked. This is common when fishing upstream because flies get lodged above rocks. When you walk or reach around to free it, let the line loose. If you keep it tight as you go around, it has a tendency to stay hooked.

If you are hooked to a rock that is above the surface, a roll cast will pull the fly from the other direction, and the fly will come free four out of five times. This maneuver, however, seldom works when flies are hooked to submerged rocks or wood.

Releasing flies from wood is difficult because the hook is embedded in the material. Usually it's necessary to physically unhook the fly. This can often be done with the rod. Recently I was fishing to a crowd of rising fish when I hooked a stick on the edge of the pool. I would have spooked the fish had I gone all the way down to the snag to unhook the fly by hand. Instead, I slipped up to within 12 feet—the length of my arm and rod—and ran the rod tip right down on the snag. I then pulled the fly up tight to the tip-top eye by taking up the entire leader into the rod. A little jiggle and push in the other direction, and the fly was free. The fish thought the brown rod was just

Save that Poundmeister! Slide the tip top over the embedded fly, hold the line tight, and push. *Wes Edling*

another stick and kept rising. I dried the fly off and caught a 17-inch brown on the next cast.

This handy trick saves flies and soaked shirtsleeves, too. It is especially helpful when nymphing snag-infested waters. Most strike indicators won't fit through the guides, however, so if you find yourself snagging on the bottom a lot, use the flat roll-on indicators. Although this technique might seem dangerous duty for your rod tip, I have never seen a rod broken when used this way.

Whether beginner or expert, we all hook many a tree. I often supply flies when guiding, and because I hate tying the things, I equally disdain decorating the forest with them. Consequently, I have become quite the expert on the holding qualities of various plants. The severity of the snag is dependent on the species of tree that has attracted the fly. When hooked to a pine, spruce, or fir, I usually just break the fly off without tricks or ceremony. Those trees don't like to let go, although ponderosas are more amenable to catch-and-release. When your fly lands in a soft wood, it has a decent chance of coming out if you don't pull it up snug. Instead, snap, snap, snap with sharp little jerks. If you are hooked to a dead branch, snap it repeatedly at a right angle to the branch. The branch has a better chance of breaking when yanked on from that direction.

When snagged with sinking lines, try pointing the rod straight at the fly, then take the line in your hand and pull. When just shy of the breaking point, let go. The line will spring forward enough to pull the fly from the other direction—and occasionally let it go.

SECURE THE FLY

There are many ways to keep your fly while walking between fishing spots. I simply stick my fly in the "keeper" and reel in tight. (For years I would just stick it in the cork and ruined the handles on all my rods.) The problem with putting it in the keeper is that you that have to some-how manually pull the line out of the rod to start a new cast.

But there are elaborate ways to secure the fly so that the fly line is actually out of the rod and ready for the next cast. You can run the leader around the reel and then hook the fly in a guide halfway up the rod. And when it comes time to cast, pull a little slack out, give the rod butt a tap, and the fly will fall out and instantly be in the air. That's the way it is supposed to work, and it does with some flies—but you may just get another tangle instead. In which case just stick the fly into the keeper and reel up tight.

WHEN THE END OF THE LEADER GOES BELOW THE TIP TOP

When the fly line gets sucked into the rod, you don't always have to go through the hassle of reaching for the end of the rod and pulling the line out manually. Put the fly in the current and pull it against the flow a couple of times. Doing this will usually get the fly line back out of the guides. Some outfits are more prone to this nuisance than others. Using a leader that is too long in short-line situations exacerbates this problem.

THE FEWER KNOTS, THE BETTER

Because knots are the weakest link in the chain, and tying them cuts down on actual fishing time, using simpler knots is a good idea. An improved clinch knot is okay, but the 16-20 is better—especially for fluorocarbon—and after some practice very fast to tie.

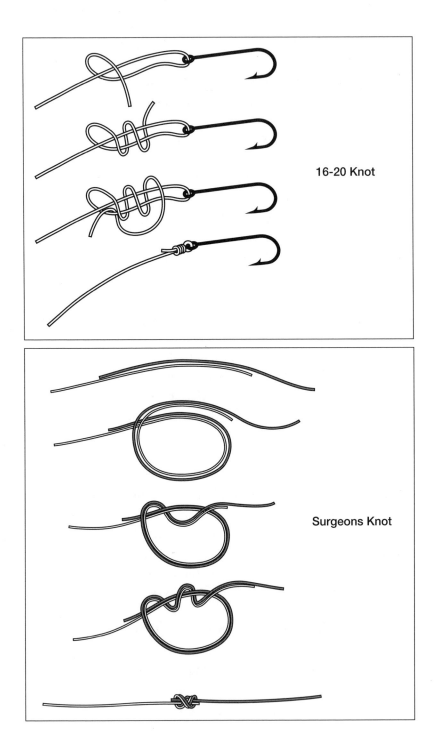

16-20 Knot

Surgeons Knot

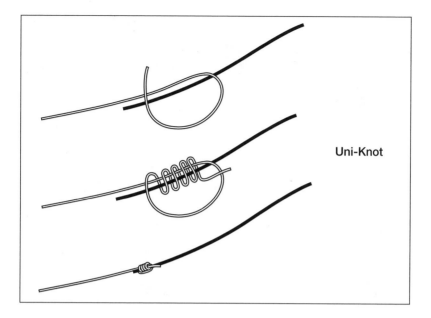

Uni-Knot

TYING A TWO-FLY SETUP

Every other person I guide asks whether I tie my second fly from the eye or the bend of the hook. I have finally found something I don't have a strong opinion about! But if I were pressed to make a choice, I'd go with the eye. I have seen—on rare occasions—the knot slip off the bend of a barbless hook.

But when fishing multiple wet flies that are going to be retrieved, tie the additional flies to the bend of the hook so that they swim straight.

DON'T WALK AND FISH SIMULTANEOUSLY

I'm often guilty of this, and I imagine I've missed a few thousand trout because of it. When you finish fishing a spot, stop to examine the water ahead for the next attractive fishing location and, just as important, for the best place from which to fish it. Remember that your first cast into a spot is by far the one most likely to get a hit, but if a haphazard cast is made before you get into proper position, the fly may drag over the fish and spook it. Don't fish while you're moving. It's sloppy business, you won't be ready if you get a strike, and the motions of casting and wading simultaneously send alarming wakes that alert the trout.

When fishing slower waters stay back from the bank and travel slow and quiet, then ease into position and make your cast.

By approaching this still pool from the side—with the sun behind him—this angler has fooled a nice trout.

HEADS OR TAILS

In smaller streams you may not want to approach long, still pools from below. The fish in the shallow water at the tail of the pool are usually smaller trout. But if alarmed they will run upstream and alert their larger cousins. So, instead of spooking the whole pool, take to the bank well below the pool, slip around, and approach the head of the pool from the side. The bigger trout will most likely be there, and because the water will be deeper and broken, you will be less visible to the fish.

ROCKY LIES

Feeding trout often sit in the cushion right in front of big rocks. When a submerged fly gets close to a boulder, most anglers whip it to the surface well upstream of the spot and miss a good opportunity. Let the fly get close to the rock and then, by lifting the rod slowly, ease the fly out of the water right in front of the boulder. That way the trout will have a chance to catch it.

Don't whip flies to the surface at the end of drift—let this guy catch one.

HOT AND COLD ADVICE

Cold winter and hot summer conditions present challenges and solutions.

For example, excellent fly fisher Justin Spence taught me that when I'm fishing in the winter, I should spray aerosol cooking oil on my rod's guides to keep them from icing up.

When it's hot, clean your eyeglasses in soapy water before you fish, and they won't fog up. When fishing in salt water, carry a clean hand towel in a sealed bag to clean sunglasses. Stay cool by keeping a wet towel around your head. In very hot weather, wear absorbent clothes—and take a dip every now and then.

I put on sunscreen a couple of times a day. I also wear long sleeves and sun gloves—which are also great for bugs and brush. Don't put sunscreen on your forehead because if you sweat, it runs into your eyes. One of the new scarf buffs that you can pull up to cover your face is great for protecting your lips from the sun. If you have trouble with your lips burning, use a lip balm with zinc oxide. If you can't find the lip stuff, you can buy straight zinc oxide at the pharmacy.

DEHOOKING PEOPLE

I have witnessed a lot of humans hooked, and I have noticed that getting impaled isn't as bad as staying impaled; it's wearing the fly that bothers

When the victim is hooked with a large fly, a loop of mono or other heavy line will allow you to pull the hook straight back.

people. Whether a doctor or a fisher removes the fly, it has to come out nearly the same way it went in, and the operation might as well be performed sooner rather than later.

I would like to share with you a system of unhooking people that I have used over the years. The first step is to cut the leader above the fly. As I'm doing this, I start the psychological phase of the operation by explaining the options: "We could leave this great fishing spot and go to the emergency room." That aims the patient's thinking in the right direction. Next I explain a gruesome method of hook removal that we are not going to use: "We could run it all the way through, cut the point off with pliers, and then back it out." That description makes the patient anxious for more options and ready for the final step. In a gentle voice I say, "If we were releasing one of those lovely trout that we hooked this morning . . .," and as I tenderly get hold of the fly right at the bend, I yank straight back. There is but one chance to do this, so it must be done with authority.

Part of the fun is viewing the abrupt emotional swings in the emancipated patient. Bug-eyed shock turns to relief in seconds. When the victim is hooked with a large fly or snagged in the delicates, you should think about using a piece of monofilament to remove the fly. The mono allows the hook to be pulled straight back.

ANOTHER USE FOR DUCT TAPE

Duct tape is marvelous for temporarily patching waders made of most materials, although not neoprene. It works so well that I usually forget to patch the things properly and walk around with the tape on my high-dollar waders for half the season.

It is great to have a few inches of duct tape in your vest to reattach the reel seat on your rod. From my experience, the more expensive the rod, the likelier it is to have the reel seat come unglued.

MISCELLANEOUS ITEMS

Whether you use a vest or a pack, you should carry several other light-weight nonfishing items: insect repellent, extra Chapstick, sunscreen, lighter, tiny flashlight, toilet paper, first aid kit (or at least Band-Aids), and superglue. Don't forget to put your camera and cell phone into a zip-lock bag.

Whenever you buy some sort of little doodad for fishing—glasses, camera case, wallet, or fly box—get the bright-colored one so that you can find it when you lose it in the grass.

After all your gear has been tallied and touted—whether carried in a vest or pack—it adds up to a sore back.

OH, MY ACHING BACK

The weight of all that junk, when combined with the horrible posture we adopt in our bent-over intensity, can give us a hell of a backache. My late, great friend Gene Berry wrote with near-scientific insight, in an article entitled "The Fisherman's Awful Secret," that the pronounced stoop of fisher folk is actually a sign that we fishers are a yet-to-be-advanced subspecies of human—not yet fully erect.

Being a prime example of this stooped primate, I have had a back-ache all my life, and after fishing for awhile I get on the lookout for a log lying about 3 feet off the ground that I can bend backward on for a few

Stumped, stooped, and stymied—Taos Fly Shop guides lose a big one.

minutes. (Wooden fences and bridge rails of proper height also work.) I
stretch one side and then the other, relieving and elongating the spine,
hopefully sending this slouched and stooped fisherman toward full stat-
ure in the animal kingdom.

No surprise that we fishers are a lethargic and forgetful lot as well.
Whenever you take your naps and stretches, make it a habit to look
around afterward to rescue anything that fell out of your pockets.

BLACKENED TROUT

We normally release trout, but occasionally it can be good to keep them.
For instance, in some places the trout are so small and numerous that
culling midsize ones will give the larger fish room to grow. If you want
to munch some while you're on the water but don't have any cooking
gear handy, try my "blackened trout" recipe. (The modern catch-and-
release fly fisher may not have much experience killing a trout. Hold it
near the tail and whack its head on a rock to dispatch it.)

Impale one gutted 8-inch trout on a green willow stick inserted into
its mouth. Place it onto a roaring fire; "roaring" is the key word here.
Don't wait for coals to form. Remove the trout before the willow stick
burns up—about three minutes. You will know that the trout is done
when the fins are burned off and the fish has been sufficiently "blackened." Add lemon and salt if you have them.

LEADERS

Many fly fishermen (yes, men are the gender in question on this issue,
too) seem to have "issues" with leaders and can be seen fussing with
leader wallets or compulsively snapping broccoli rubber bands that bind
thick wads of the precious things. If you are so afflicted, you might start
rehabilitation by throwing away those leaders that are a couple of years
old. If that feels good, then toss the long and light ones (anything over
9 feet and thinner than 5X). "Braided" ones must certainly go as well.

When guiding I *never* trust the terminal end of a client's rig because
it will invariably be too long, too thin, too thick, and not end in fluorocarbon. Although there are leader setups for flat water and other special-
ized fishing situations, 90 percent of trout fishing can be accomplished

with a 7 1/2-foot leader *and* the addition of a fluorocarbon tippet. If you have various tippet diameters in your pocket, you can reconstruct your leader as needed. (Now that you have tossed the leaders, replace with spools of tippet from 0 to 6X—4X and thinner should be fluorocarbon.) You should be able to fish many outings with the same leader if you rebuild it as needed.

In the first edition of this book I suggested attaching leader to line by knot, but the loops that are at the end of fly lines now are very good. They actually help float the line because they are closed cell, and water doesn't penetrate the end.

FLUOROCARBON

Although there were years of inconsistent behavior from fluorocarbon, manufacturers have got it down now. We often hear complaints in the shop about the price, but anglers fail to take into account that because you can hardly break the stuff, you don't use much of it. And with fluoro you don't break flies off. You get tired of looking at them, actually. Straightened hooks are a problem.

4

Casting

An endless number of in-depth books have been written on casting, so I'm not going to try to explain the mechanics. But having watched and helped thousands of folks cast, I do have some observations that might be helpful.

LESSONS

First off, it is important to take casting lessons, hopefully at the beginning of your fly-fishing career. Self-taught casters develop bad habits that can become deeply ingrained and hard to correct. A fly cast is just as challenging to learn as a good golf swing; but whereas golfers get lessons, most fly casters wing it—rather literally, I fear. Or they get instruction from relatives who "know how to fly fish."

The first question I asked my students in my guides school last year was, "How many of you have had casting lessons?" Of the dozen well-experienced fly fishers, nobody raised a hand. And sure enough, they had all faults covered. After several days of casting instruction from us, we got everyone making longer and more accurate casts. But it can take years to untrain one's self and develop a more efficient stroke.

I was a self-taught and ugly caster until I got help from two great instructors, the late Mel Krieger and Mike Atwell. Personally, I could not have changed my casting without an instructor holding my wrist and physically showing me a proper casting motion. Since then my casting instruction is so much about feel that I have students keep their eyes closed while learning some of the motions.

SCHOOLS

There are many ways to learn to cast, but a school with personalized, hands-on instruction over the course of several consecutive days is the best. I used to give brief casting lessons to my guiding clients before we set out to fish for the day. But catching fish is the goal on a guided trip, and although a caster may improve with on-the-water instruction, such an abbreviated effort doesn't sink in, and the client will usually forget it all when he or she sees a trout jump.

Although a fly-fishing school will cover many areas of the sport, casting is certainly the most important aspect that people take home with them. We have found, from years of conducting schools, that everyone learns differently and that one student will benefit from one type of instruction, whereas another may learn from another type.

Being both technically and intellectually challenged, I have a kinetic style of instruction that I have come by from years of guiding. My guides have their own forms of teaching. Casting lessons should be spread out over a period of time because the mind and muscles seem to lose concentration after an hour or so.

Part of schooling casters is putting them in on-the-water situations that instruct. If we find fish feeding under trees, for instance, a typical beginning caster will usually throw a loop that is too wide and put the fly in the tree the first few times. But with coaching, the student—now attentive with a fish nearby—listens. And when a nice tight loop finally skips under the branch, and a trout eats the fly, self-imposed barriers crumble, instincts takes over, and a fly caster is born.

Something that really stands out, after guiding thousands of fly fishers, is that most people know only one type of cast—usually mid-range. But several casts should be in every angler's repertoire. And casts such as the roll cast and tip cast will teach you much about the casting stroke.

PICK UP AND LAY DOWN

I often use the "pick up and lay down" exercise to teach casting. The caster makes one backcast and then lays down the forward cast. It is a good beginner tool, but don't make it a habit because we run into people who have had too much of this and think that it is false casting. (False casting occurs when the line stays in the air.) If you hit the water on every stroke, you are going to spook all the trout.

THE ROLL CAST

The late Mel Krieger taught me how to roll-cast *a long way*. In his book *The Essence of Flycasting,* he says that the roll cast "is a method of flycasting in which line is rolled forward without a backcast. We use this cast to present a fly when obstacles, like trees or rocks or even a strong following wind, prevent a normal backcast."

He also mentions that "the roll cast plays an important role in flycasting . . . and the development of a good flycasting stroke." The roll cast is a big part of my casting instructions because the movements that comprise a regular cast are the same and can be studied in slow motion. Although the roll cast has to be performed on still water, some indoor practice rods will roll-cast well on carpet and are superb tools for learning to cast.

If you have trouble with the roll cast, be aware that some rods roll-cast a lot better than others. An outfit that is underlined (meaning the line is light for the rod) will roll-cast poorly. Although it may appear simple, this cast is difficult to perform well, and even the most experienced fly caster has trouble doing it perfectly every time. For specific instructions, go to Mel's book or video.

CIMARRON SLING

We guide a lot of trips here in northern New Mexico on a small tailwater stream named the Cimarron. Narrow and brush lined, it holds many trout, but unfortunately they're best caught with a two-fly setup. Because false casts and tight loops catch lots more branches than trout, the best cast is an ugly short stroke—a half-cast/half-roll that starts with a half-assed water load.

This cast is performed by letting the flies drift past you and then, just before they get tight in the current, slinging them forward with a rounded-out half stroke. I don't know if it would be more accurate to call this gruesome move a roll cast or just plain flailing, but most beginners take to it right away.

The flies—a dry/dropper set—travel vertically and at an angle that keeps them just in the midstream canopy and usually out of the trees. Such a cast descends with slack, allowing for a good float in the fast, choppy water. Because this is always a very short line situation, a good hook set is still possible because a sweep of the rod will take up all the slack. Even when standing midstream the angler is almost always in the shade and thereby undetected. And given the quick and choppy pace of the stream, fish may take at your feet.

FOLLOWING WIND ROLL CAST

In the rivers in Argentina, the wind blows upstream most of the time at a pretty vigorous clip. Backcasting into it is work—especially if you're using the large, wind-resistant dry fly and nymph favored there. Although inaccurate, the easiest way to get the flies upstream is with a wind-*assisted* cast that launches them skyward. This is accomplished by making a roll cast and then extending the arm up at the end of the stroke, aiming upward. The idea is that you're rounding out the loop and getting more line airborne. Many of the more typical casting faults—using too much wrist, coming back too far, and reaching at the end of the stroke—may be of assistance here. Experiment with casting faults in the wind.

BAD SHOULDER

I have a shoulder injury, and at one point I couldn't bring my arm up to where it needed to go to get a good backcast or even double haul. So I learned that I could get extra power by shooting a few feet of the line out the backcast, then stopping the rod sharply. This loads the hell out of the rod with little effort and minimal use of the arms and shoulders.

THE TIP CAST

A big trout rises a few feet away. You try to put the fly onto the fish's head, but first it lands to port and, with the next cast, to the fish's starboard side. Before you know it, the prize has been spooked or wandered out of range without ever seeing the fly. Few fly fishermen can throw the tight loop necessary to make short, accurate casts. They bring the rod back too far or snap the wrist at the wrong time. The only way to get that sweet loop is by flexing the rod tip. The key to accomplishing that is learning the little snap of the wrist that flexes just the tip. Learning

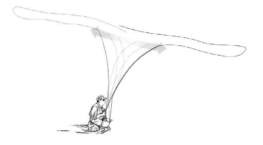

If you really want to learn how to cast, keep it short and on target. But note that a tighter loop here would create a tailing loop and its subsequent wind knot. Wind knots are also caused by a snappy and/or constrained casting motion. The casting stroke should be made with a smooth acceleration of power. And the arm should move on a vertical, not horizontal, plane.

the tip cast is not easy, but it is the key to all good casts. All casts—long, short, curved—are about bending the rod. A complete caster can utilize the entire rod, from the butt right up to the tip. But the tip is the trickiest section to bend, and if you learn to flex it, the rest of your casting will fall into place.

Having an instructor physically show you is, of course, best, but if you can't get a lesson, here's a helpful exercise that will teach you this cast instinctively. Place a target 15 to 30 feet away, tie an inch of bright yarn onto the end of your leader, and try to hit the target consistently. Your backcast should be very short and straight over your head. When I start folks on this drill, it isn't long before they ignore the target and start shooting line "a way out yonder." They seem so pleased with themselves that I hate to burst their bubble and tell them midrange casting is easy. If you really want to improve, stay on target with the short cast. This exercise will cause you to tighten your loop and teach you that all-important flick of the wrist. It's the only way you will hit the target consistently.

THE MIDRANGE CAST

The midrange cast delivers flies medium distances and is used for a lot of trout fishing. During the casting stroke the rod flexes in the middle because it is brought from the old 10 to 2 o'clock position. With the powerful rods of this day and age, the angle is really more like 10:30 to 1:30. This cast is fine for throwing one or two unweighted flies, but when other items are attached to your leader, such as strike indicators and weight, the cast needs to be modified.

SLINGING LEAD

If you are slinging lead, a regular cast will get you lots of tangles. When all that junk is cast with a tight loop, the weight and air resistance make the terminal tackle collapse onto the line, creating a mess.

The solution is to make the cast in an arc but with everything tight and no slack spots in the leader to cause trouble. The rod tip should actually go in an oval rather than in the usual straight line. Start the cast with a snap that is strong enough that line has sufficient power to complete the loop. Grab a piece of rope and sling it around and around cowboy-style over your head. Then envision what it would take to do this with a fly rod. It's a similar motion.

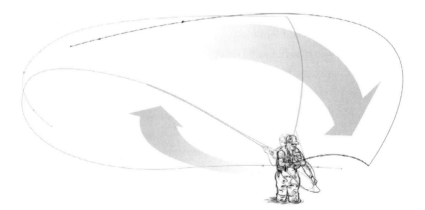

When slinging lead, start the cast with a motion that is powerful enough that the "junk" will sail around on a tight line.

An oval casting motion slices into the wind better than a standard cast.

THE BIG CAST

While spending several years in the Bahamas chasing bonefish over the breezy flats, I learned that an oval motion sends the fly into the wind better than a traditional overhead cast. The oval, however, should not be as pronounced as the oval used for casting the nymph rig. When the cast is properly executed, the line will pass underneath your casting arm on the backcast and above the rod on the forecast, as a traditional cast would.

This is accomplished by bringing the arm back lower on the backcast than you normally would.

While guiding in the salt I discovered that most clients, accustomed to casting for dainty trout, couldn't generate enough power to get any distance. They had never learned to bend the rod right down to the handle. I would have the same problem at the beginning of each saltwater fly-fishing season, and it always took a couple of weeks before I developed a powerful stroke. All trout fishermen should do a lot of practicing well before any seaside adventure. Even better, have somebody show you how.

THE CURVED CAST

The curved cast is another important tool for the stream fly fisher. For example, a fisherman may be standing in the slow water on the inside of

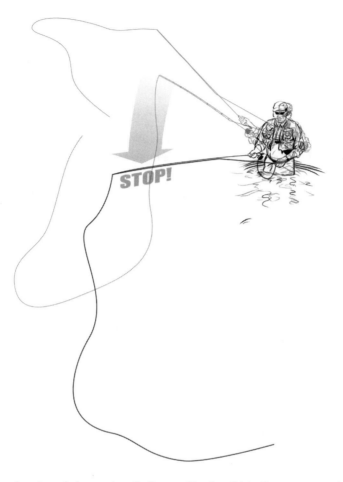

A curved cast can help you drop fly, line, and leader all into the same current—
giving you a good float.

a bend, and the fish are in the current just off the bank. A straight-line
cast will put most of the line and leader into the slower water, and only
the fly will drop into the faster water. Consequently, you get a very short
float because the part that is in the faster water quickly swings around
and drags. You will get a better drift if everything is in the same speed
of current.

Although wading into a more favorable position is the best option,
this isn't always possible, making a curved cast the next-best solution. It

is done by making a powerful sidearm cast and stopping the rod short. This shocks the rod and sends the end of the line, leader, and fly around in a curve. Many anglers have difficulty with this cast because they don't have a cast that is strong enough to overpower the forward stroke.

THE BAD CAST

Unfortunately, the bad cast comes naturally for a lot of folks. It's actually a great tool to use when fishing upstream on fast-falling creeks where only short casts are required. The bad cast is easy enough; just perform one of several casting infractions: break your wrist, reach, or best of all, don't put any snap into the forward stroke. Doing that will bring the rod down flat, which takes the bend out of the rod and puts slack into the line and leader, giving you a longer drag-free float than a proper straight cast would.

BOTHERSOME SHOCKED CASTS

Another somewhat common problem occurs when a nymph curves around when a cast that is too forceful "shocks" on the final stroke. The line comes tight, and a heavily weighted fly will zing around in a curve. The drift will start out with slack so a fish may take, but you won't know anything about it. All that junk should be cast smoothly so that it lies out straight. It's done by taking the snap out of the final stroke and softening the delivery. It also helps to release a foot or two of line when the cast is landing. If the cast does hit the water with unwanted slack, pull on the line to straighten it out.

BACKHANDING

When fishing upstream it is best for a right-hander to be on the left side of the river. That way the cast falls to your right, and you can fish the drift out

When fishing up the "wrong side" of a stream, backhand the cast.

with the rod staying in that comfortable position. Stream geography, how-ever, often places you on the other side of the river. This is a more awkward position because the line will drift down on the side of you opposite the rod, and you will have to fish across your body. If you use a conventional over-the-shoulder cast in this situation, you will make a cross-current pre-sentation. You can mend to improve the drift, but mending should always be a last resort, and it is usually better to backhand the cast.

THREE BACKHAND CASTS

Backhanding drops your cast at a more favorable angle, giving you more of a straight upstream presentation. It also puts the rod in a better posi-tion to start the drift, and your line, leader, and fly will be in the same current. There are three ways to backhand the cast. These can best be described by how the rod is held, referring to the position of the thumb.

(Keep in mind that the proper grip on the rod is with the thumb on top of the handle, opposite the guides.)

The first way to backhand a cast is with the thumb up. This is the most common way anglers backhand a cast, but it is a weak stroke

Few anglers are aware of how they backhand a cast. Most do it with the thumb up, as shown. *Wes Edling*

The No. 2 backhand cast is good for casting dries at relatively close range.
Wes Edling

because the arm and shoulder can't get into the motion. Consequently the rod is merely waved in front, and the delivery will pile up. Try this motion, and the others to be described, with your hand now. You'll get a better idea of the points made here.

The second way to backhand a cast is by bringing the backcast over your left shoulder, understanding that all these directions are for right-handers and that the opposite is true for lefties. The thumb should come straight toward and almost touch the left shoulder. This cast is best for short-distance accuracy because the forward stroke is much the same as a conventional cast, where you are looking and aiming at your target. Incidentally, you can get more power out of the cast if you lean back on the backcast. That gives you a longer stroke and consequently a more powerful cast.

The third backhand cast gives you by far the most power, but accuracy is sacrificed. This cast is done with the thumb facing right, like a hitchhiker's. Technically, this is not a backhand cast but rather a conventional sidearm stroke, where the backcast is used as the forecast. I have had good luck teaching this by instructing anglers to turn around and pretend that they are casting downstream. I tell them to look back

A sidearm cast, with the thumb horizontal, generates a lot of power. When backhanding use your backcast as the forward cast. *Wes Edling*

upstream when they drop the cast. This is a powerful motion because the whole arm and shoulder are behind the rod and driving it. Incidentally, this is also a handy cast for when the wind is blowing at a right angle into your casting arm. Just turn around and use the backcast as the forecast, and it will put the line on the lee side of your body and prevent your getting hooked.

THE WATER LOAD

The water load is the ticket if you are fishing tight streams with brush on the banks. The advantage is that the fly spends very little time in the air, where the troublesome trees lurk. It is a good cast to use when a sunken fly has drifted below you because in such a situation you already have enough line out for the next drift, and you needn't make a false cast. Let the current do the work. When the line straightens out below you, it loads the rod, and line, leader, tippet, and fly can be flung back upstream with an easy motion. The rod should be angled well back toward the fly but not quite at it. Then the submerged fly should be lifted slowly to the surface by raising the rod. When the weight of the line is felt pulling steadily against the rod, a smooth and easy stroke will send it upstream. If brush is a problem, the cast can be kept very low to the water. People often put too much energy into this lob. To maximize

When waterloading, a smooth and easy motion sends the fly back upstream best.

its effectiveness, make sure that the fly is at the surface when you start the stroke.

A water load makes a fly's destination generally hit-or-miss, but it *can* be an accurate cast—and in tight quarters it is the way to go. Do it by visually measuring the amount of line hanging downstream from the rod, and compare that with the distance to the target. Look back and forth—like how a golfer measures a putt—and remember to always err short when in doubt.

LEFT-RIGHT FINESSE

When a right-hander is fishing upstream to his left, the fly drifts down on the left side, and it's awkward to start a new cast from that position. Why? Because the fly is on the left, the rod is on the right, and the angler will be bringing the fly across his body, putting himself in the precarious position of possibly hooking himself when he starts his cast. If you find yourself in this situation, you can get out of the predicament ever so gracefully by putting the rod over your head. Start with the rod to your left, swing it back around until it ends up pointed over your right shoulder, and then proceed with the next cast. Do this slowly so that the fly has a chance to drift away from you. Think of yourself as a cowboy throwing a rope, making a circle over your head.

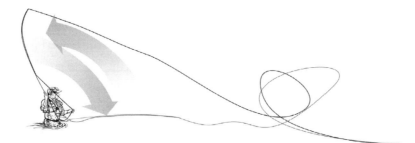

If you find yourself with too much slack line, start your cast with a roll cast to get the line off the water.

ANOTHER HELPFUL CAST

Here is another slick move that can keep you and your guide from getting hooked and tangled with fly and line. If you are fishing upstream, as most anglers do, with too much slack and try to start a new cast, the result can be reckless and sloppy. Rectify the situation by making a little forward flip or roll cast to get the line into the air and under control. When the roll cast straightens out in front of you, it loads the rod for the backcast.

THE LIFT-AND-SNAP

When casting and retrieving a short and fixed amount of line—when paralleling a bank from a boat, for instance—it is usually most productive to retrieve a fly just a few feet and then snap it back to the structure where the fish are. If you strip it in every time, you will waste a lot of time false casting and remeasuring the distance. Then the cast will likely be too short or too long anyway. It is much more efficient to use the same amount of line each cast and retrieve it just a few feet by *lifting the rod*. When the rod gets vertical, make one crisp backcast and snap it back at the same premeasured distance.

CRITIQUE YOUR CAST

You can judge your own casting if you not only watch it but also listen to it. A rod that is properly cast makes very little sound; a rod that doesn't bend, however, makes a whooshing noise. An equally sinister

That's too far back!

sight accompanies this audio atrocity—that of the fly and leader unrolling after the line is on the water.

TOO FAR BACK!

A common problem with casters is breaking the wrist and bringing the rod back too far. I have repeated the phrase, "Too far back!" to thousands of fly fishers in my life, with usually little more to show for it than a wrinkled brow and sore throat. My frustration has forced me to develop a new casting exercise that is extreme and controversial but a foolproof way of correcting this most common of casting faults. All that is required is a very expensive fly rod and a fence that stands 3 or 4 feet higher than you. Simply stand 1 or 2 feet in front of the fence, with your back to it, and then proceed to cast. Your backcast should sail over the fence. (Here I insert my disclaimer that neither I nor the publisher is responsible for broken fly rods. If your rod breaks against the fence, rest assured that you went "too far back.")

FLOATING ARM

The floating arm and shoulder are a common problem with the self-taught and can cause the whooshing sound. Instead of anchoring the rod, the caster pushes the rod back and forth on a horizontal plane and doesn't bend the rod. Doing this accomplishes little beyond giving the caster's upper arm and shoulder a mighty workout. The caster's body rocks to and fro when he has to cast any distance, and if he's in the water his little dance will send alarming waves in all directions. A good casting stroke is more up and down than front and back. The rod should be pulled downward rather than pushed forward.

REACHING

Many, if not most, fly fishers "reach" at the end of the cast. (Lefty Kreh told me I do it, too!) I have also noticed that the reacher is often guilty of too much false casting. He wings the line back and forth with greater intensity on each stroke. When the laydown is anticipated, he sabotages it by reaching out with the arm. The subconscious is at work

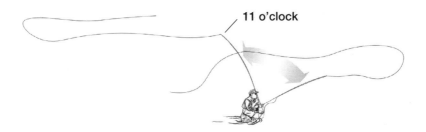

11 o'clock

When casting in a wind, shift your casting stroke from the 10 to 2 o'clock range to 11 to 3 o'clock. This will break the cast right over the water, and the wind can't play with the fly.

here, telling the caster that reaching will get him more distance. The opposite is true: Power is lost when the arm is extended at the end of the cast.

It is easy to tell if you are a reacher: Just see where your arm is positioned when the cast is completed. If your elbow is down and the rod is straight out in front you at the conclusion of the cast, you've done it right. If your arm ends up extended, you've done it wrong. I'm forever correcting casters while they are fishing. Helping them to get rid of the reach is not too hard, but it tends to creep back with each stroke, and after a few minutes the arm ends up extended again.

Another common fault is that most casters have far too little range of motion and cramp their cast into a short stroke where their hand travels only a foot or so. If your casts don't turn over all the way, or if they come down hard, this may be the cause. If you can learn to let the arm ride upward, it will open up your stroke and improve your casting immensely.

Some anglers have the bad habit of holding and casting the fly rod with the index finger, rather than the thumb, on top of the handle. They learned to do this because it was hard to break their wrist if their index finger was on top—an honorable enough reason. But when a really powerful cast is needed, the index finger doesn't have strength enough to do the job.

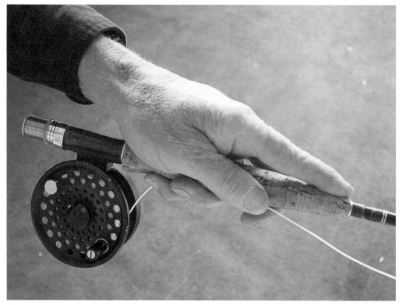

This position may be okay in making short, accurate casts but is inadequate for longer throws. *Wes Edling*

Proper hand position with thumb up and line under middle finger. *Wes Edling*

TOO MANY FINGERS

Many anglers, including some very good ones, use the index finger to pick up line. That is the finger that we naturally use for such work, but because the finger supports the rod, the grip is sometimes compromised when using it. Although it may take some time getting used to, the middle finger will do a better job. It is easier to find the line with the longer appendage, and the hand's position on the handle is not altered when reaching for the line.

TAKING UP THE SLACK

A common fault of inexperienced fly fishers in picking up slack—and playing fish—is reaching above the "pickup finger" to grab the line. Doing this wastes a lot of effort because the line needs to be constantly repositioned under the pickup finger. Strikes are missed because the line is taken up in awkward little jerks, and half the time the fingers are out of position to set the hook. When you grab the line from below the pickup finger, you are always ready to set the hook. Just clamp down on the line with the middle finger and drive the steel home.

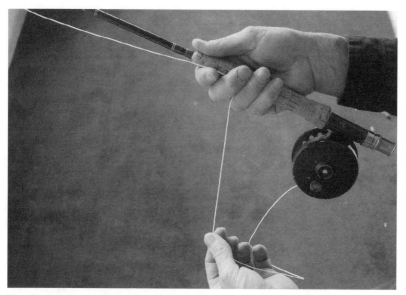

Your hands should be in this position when taking up slack line.

CHUCKING A SPOON

Another casting indiscretion is the spoon-chucking, wrist-snapping motion commonly found in those who have learned to spin cast before they ever touched a fly rod. As a casting instructor I sometimes find it impossible to convince a person—or his or her arm, which may have a mind of its own—that the fly is just not going to sail out there on a flick of the wrist. In fly casting we are, of course, casting the weight of the line. The fly is simply along for the ride. You can make a cast with just the wrist—as half of all fly casters do. It just takes a lot more work to get it out there. The arm needs to be employed. Equating a fly cast with a tennis or golf swing is much closer to what you are looking for than hurling a bass lure.

Wait for your false cast. Modern times in America have produced a new sort of fly-casting problem. Some folks are in such a hurry to have fun that they don't wait for the line to straighten out when false casting. It takes longer than you think for that line to straighten out behind you, so wait.

5

The Trout

RAINBOWS

Wild rainbows can often be identified when hooked. They instantly jump or have a powerful surge that pen-raised fish don't have. They also tend to be brighter in color, and most of the smaller wild ones are decorated with "par markings," which appear as faint fingerprints on the side. (Private hatcheries are now raising trout that look pretty wild.) These par markings fade as the fish get older but usually are visible until the fish are 10 to 12 inches. Another telltale sign of a wild rainbow is its pink fins with white tips.

Rainbow trout prosper where there are profuse food sources. They tend to occupy and feed in the main channels and riffles of rivers where such food is funneled. They feed better in warmer waters than other trout. Both rainbows and cuts are spring spawners.

Rainbow

Cutthroat

CUTTHROAT

One of the native fish of the Rockies, cutthroat have been almost entirely displaced by introduced rainbows, browns, and brookies. Like rainbows, cutthroat are spring spawners. Hybridization with rainbows created the vigorous cutbow. With all the rainbow influence there are few pure cutthroat fisheries left. They are generally a gullible fish and usually easy to catch—but they can be trained to be difficult. We fish one well-used stream where they spit out a fly faster than you can set the hook.

BROOK TROUT

Due to their equally nonaggressive temperaments, cuts and brook trout coexist well. Finding the two together in a stream is a treat. Brookies are originally native to the eastern United States but have been introduced everywhere. They are a small fish of cold-water habitats. Anything over 12 inches is good sized in the United States. Their superior flavor and propensity toward overpopulation often make their consumption environmentally sensible. Brookies and browns are autumn spawners.

Brook trout

BROWN TROUT

Originally a product of the U.K. and Germany, brown trout are probably the most respected of the trout species. They take advantage of all opportunities and when called upon can hide about anywhere and eat about anything—but often under the cover of darkness. This is a fish with a proclivity toward unrestrained aggression. In my book *Man vs. Fish—The Fly Fisherman's Eternal Struggle* I have a story and photos of a 4-pound brown I caught in Argentina that latched onto a 10-inch rainbow and *wouldn't* let go! Although it was never hooked I teased it ashore until it beached itself. It would seem as if these fish don't feed in

Brown trout

the warmth of summer, but if you find a place where they have not been fished for, they may greedily eat anyway.

STOCKED TROUT

I tend to think of stocked trout as a distinctly different species. But I know what the reader is thinking—let's just skip this section because we fly fishers are nature boys and antistocker. But before aspersions are cast, let me mention that we hear this complaint much more away from the water—not when one of these chastised fish is actually tugging on the line. In fact, it is rare indeed for any fly fishers—even those very experienced—to inquire whether a fish they just caught was stocked or not. Some of the rainbows we catch in our neck of the woods have been stocked, and in lakes they are almost always stocked because natural trout reproduction is rare in lakes. Stockers can usually be identified by their damaged fins, frayed from contact with the walls of their cage.

"Holdovers" are those stockers that survive a winter. In some waters the carryover is uncommon, and in others the fish are expected to survive. After two years they are close to the wild and quite spunky. It is a shame that few stocked trout have the genes to live long. I am not a biologist, but it would seem that if the offspring of these stronger hold-over fish were propagated, there would be far more survival. But there is little motivation for that because state fishery departments are happy to release dumb and listless trout because the fish are then more easily caught by licensed-buying masses of anglers.

As our waters become more used and abused, stocked trout become more important. And not just for "put and take." Stocking is also a tool to furnish fishing in good catch-and-release fisheries. A river in southern Colorado—the Conejos—has a fine population of nice-size brown trout. The magic time to catch them is about two weeks at the end of runoff when profuse caddis, stonefly, and green drake mayfly hatches occur. These old trout, once fooled each year, become hard to fool again, and that makes for a very short season there. We fish a couple of private pieces of the river where large rainbows are augmented in early summer. True, this is synthetic and self-serving for the fisherman; and the stockers no doubt compete with, and ultimately reduce, the wild fish. But these plantings maintain the quality of fishing until the browns dumb up again in the autumn.

Stocked trout usually stay close to where they are put, and if they are planted in slow water they may remain there until extracted by humans or, in some cases, other animals. I once stayed on a river in Idaho and had the best birding imaginable when a truckload of stocker was put into a slow pool by my cabin. A dozen osprey arrived, and there was a constant bombardment from the birds perched in the branches of a dead tree right over the fish. Unlike wild trout and fly-fishing guides—most of whom will go miles for food or sex—the stockers stay close to where they are put. Of those that move, few will travel upstream.

The stocked trout usually don't eat in the first few days, but after about day five they will come hungrily to the fly. They'll usually take a nymph over a dry and seem to prefer something a little flashy like a red or blue Copper John. After *these* fish have been caught a couple times *they* will learn to be shy like any other hunted animal.

The cost of fish is not as prohibitive as might be expected. And more and more of these larger stocked trout are showing up in public water. Pagosa Springs, Colorado, and Red River, New Mexico, stock large trout in their towns and get a lot of tourist dollars in return.

6

Water and Weather Conditions

Getting on the water when conditions are right is probably the most important ingredient in successful trout fishing. All the gear, ability, and knowledge in the world won't amount to a hill of beans if the fish are inactive. We'll never know exactly what gets them going, but the clever angler pays attention to the air and water and learns, over time, which combination of conditions produces the best fishing.

When you have to make a living outguessing Mother Nature's finicky ways, you pay really close attention. Here are some conclusions I have come to after decades of stalking the wily trout and the even more elusive greenback.

TRAVEL WITH KNOWLEDGE

Anglers who live close to their fishing should have a different plan than those who have to travel to get to the water. Folks who fish in their own neighborhood have a big advantage because they don't have to waste time pounding the stream when conditions are bad.

If you have to travel to fish, knowing what shape the river is in before you get there is of great benefit. Water conditions are forever changing: It's too high and muddy, too low and clear, too hot, too cold—always too something. So be flexible. Don't embrace rigid notions: "I'm going to fish the Big Muddy in June, dagnabbit." The Big Muddy might be too clear in June. Always have a Plan B ready.

FLOW RATE

Flow rates for rivers throughout the United States can be found by web searching "streamflow" for your state. Websites provide you with measurements from those little tin silos you see along our rivers, and it enables you not only to find the up-to-the-minute flow rate for a river

Canyon streams generally fish better when the water is low.

but also to see the trend, that is, whether the water is rising or falling and—on some—water and air temps. Of course, this type of information is of value only if you know what you're looking for. A rate of 100 cubic feet per second will be meaningless unless you know at what level the river fishes best. Call the nearest fly shop and ask what conditions their guides prefer. If you do go and find the water to your liking, check the flow rate on the website when you get home so you have a reference point for the future.

TEMPERATURE AND TIME OF DAY

If the water is warm, trout, especially the bruisers, don't feed well. If the water is too cold, the fish act like kids with a plate full of vegetables: They pick and nibble. (Although the largest trout are often the first fish to be active in the cold of early and late season.) You can have good fishing when the water is running hot or cold, however, by choosing the right time of day. I often have been on my way to fish around midmorning and run into a discouraged, tired fisherman on his way back in. He had hit the water with a vengeance at dawn. It sounds so promising to be out there before breakfast, but from my experience, the best trout fishing occurs at midday. Insects usually become active in midmorning, and the trout's appetite seems to peak at about 1 p.m. The extremely knowledgeable Roderick Haig-Brown came to the same conclusion but added another explanation for midday success. In his wonderful book, *A River Never Sleeps,* Haig-Brown wrote, "You know that a fisherman will probably do his best work then, too." I don't know about you, but I'm a little slow on the trigger at 0-dark-30.

When the air is very cool, the fish will feed late in the day, after the water has had a chance to warm. This makes for some predictable, and consequently good, fishing. The volume of a stream is a factor. Larger streams will be less affected by air temperature swings than smaller ones.

Conversely, if the weather is warmer than normal, the fish will start feeding earlier in the day. (In the heat of midsummer, that might be daybreak.)

Except in cold weather, late afternoon pretty well sucks for all fishing. Late evening is usually much more prosperous than early morning because most hatches occur then.

DIRECTION OF FLOW

The direction of flow is another consideration when planning to fish a particular river. For instance, small streams with spooky trout fish best if you have the sun at your back. Consequently, those that flow west will usually fish best in the last half of the day.

HIGH WATER

Trout don't want to battle big currents, so look for them where they can escape heavy flows, which is usually at the edges. When choosing an area to fish where water levels are high, look for sections of river with a lot of bends; the inside of these bends will have slack water and high concentrations of fish. If you are not familiar with a river, study maps and head for the bends.

When a river is rising or high, winding sections will usually provide more holding water than will straight stretches.

LOW WATER

High water tends to spread fish out toward the edges, but low water concentrates trout in holes. If air and water temperatures are high, the fish will be thick below oxygenated white water. One season on the Rio Grande in New Mexico, the water was miserably low and warm. A waterfall pool that had a half-mile of flat water on either side of it attracted every fish in the neighborhood. They were packed in like sardines. Because the Rio is a large river, the trout didn't spook from the commotion of a fish fighting, making it possible to catch one right after another.

RISING WATER

It is rare to be on the river when the water is rising rapidly due to precipitation, but trout can go on quite a rampage then because the first stages of flooding water will carry lots of debris, including food, before the water actually turns muddy. Areas that are freshly inundated with water may draw trout that are on the hunt for food.

In tailwaters, a rise in the flow will usually turn off fish. If the tailwaters have been low and the fish have been crowded in the holes, however, a rise often triggers mass appetites. But be patient because they usually shuffle around stretching their fins for a half hour or so before they start eating.

DISCOLORED WATER

Fly fishermen hate dirty and muddy water, and I'm no exception. This often says more about our attitude, however, than about the feeding habits of fish. After all, no matter the color of the water, they have to eat. Actually, water with some color to it often fishes better than clear water because trout feel safe when the water is a little murky and will venture into the shallows to feed. If there is more than 1 foot of visibility, they can find grub—and your fly—just fine. When the visibility is reduced to inches, fishing suffers as their feeding strategy changes because they are unable to see insects drifting by their lie. They will feed more on the bottom, and because they can't find much to eat, they will lose weight. Dead-drifting and jigging big, heavy, high-visibility flies, such as black or orange Krystal Flash Woolly Buggers, seem to be the best tactics in muddy water.

PRERUNOFF

We are all eager for runoff to end. But some of the best fishing is often on warm days in March or April just *before* runoff. In the Rockies it is common for the lower-elevation snows to melt in late winter, leaving just the high and north-facing snow, which doesn't melt until May. This can mean some perfect conditions on warm days in this prerunoff period. And there can be profuse caddis hatches (on the Arkansas in Colorado and Rio Grande in New Mexico), but it is a fine line between too cold and fishable. If you see snow or ice melting into the water, it is likely too cold to fish.

CLEARING AND DROPPING WATER

Water that is clearing and dropping puts trout on the feed. Often the best fishing of the season is when the spring runoff is winding down. Water temperatures are usually perfect then, and insect hatches are at their peak. In addition, the fish haven't been harassed since the previous year.

If the water level has been on the high side, tailwater fish almost always respond favorably when the river is lowered. Check flow rates on the Internet and grab the gear when the level plummets.

NORMAL FLOWS

I mention normal flows last for a reason. With logging, irrigation, grazing, years of poor fire management, and summer homes everywhere, few watersheds function the way God intended. All that abuse causes rivers to rise and fall drastically. Consequently, most waterways in the United States run at optimum, bank-to-bank levels only between flood and drought. On these joyous occasions, trout will luxuriate throughout the river.

HIGH OR LOW?

Some rivers fish well when the water is low, others when the water is high. Generally, deeper canyon streams and large rivers fish better under low-water conditions because the fish become easier to get at. Smaller, shallower watercourses usually fish best when running brim full. This is unquestionably true in the area of Argentina where I fish, from Bariloche north to the town of Alumine. The huge Lemay, Collon Cura, and Alumine rivers fish poorly when they are swollen, and the smaller rivers, like the Traful and Malleo, need plenty of fluid because the trout live under the willows and become homeless if the water shrinks back from the bank. Just like anywhere, if they have someplace better to go, they go. That is why sections of rivers in Argentina near lakes may produce poor fishing in summer; the trout move to the lakes when river conditions deteriorate.

ALTITUDE

In the areas with which I am most familiar—the steep mountains of New Mexico, Colorado, and Argentina—the altitude varies greatly, and streams blossom at different times. The cold-running waters at high elevations fish best in summer, and the waters lower down fish best in the cool seasons: spring, autumn, and even winter.

You can apply this same principle to determine where to fish during short-term weather changes. If a cold front hits, head downriver, where the water will be warmer. If the weather turns hot, go upstream. A good rule of thumb is to go where the temperature is the most comfortable for you; the fish will most likely agree with your choice.

WEATHER AND LIGHT

Weather is a big factor in any type of fishing. My notes reveal that the best fishing is on days when air temps top out at around 70 degrees. But otherwise, exactly what fishing corresponds to what weather is hard to pin down, but sometimes the air just smells fishy. This statement is not as far out as you might think because our noses work well when the air is still, humid, and overcast. Those also happen to be the best conditions for most insect hatches.

BLUE SKIES

Bright blue skies are what we fish under a lot in the southern Rockies, and although plenty of trout are caught in sunlight, fish and insects usually prefer shade. I experienced this recently on the Rio Grande. The

Rio winds through a deep canyon with vertical cliffs, and on this clear day, in the midst of a great caddis hatch, no fish were rising. We were catching trout on nymphs, but we wanted to use dries, and I knew a place where an overhanging cliff would be casting a shadow onto the river. When we got there, the few square yards of shaded water were crowded with risers.

HOT WEATHER

Although hot weather is perhaps the number one killer of fishing days, in early summer when the water is still cool, hot air can be good. But after the water warms, forget it. In this case, hot weather—especially combined with blue skies—is a guide's worst nightmare. This is mid-summer, when everyone wants to fish! The fishing can be tolerable early and late in the day, but in the endless wasteland of middle day it is a sure bet that there will be zero insect life and a corresponding amount of trout activity. If forced to fish, try a grasshopper (maybe with a small nymph below it) because that is one of the few insects active under the conditions.

Tailwater streams and/or those waters at high elevation will be less affected by hot weather. Also look for shade and stretches of river that are timbered. And although they're a sparse commodity, underwater springs can attract trout like magnets.

DUSKY LIGHT

The dusky light that trout love doesn't have to come from the setting of the sun. The same light can be found when clouds move in or when the sun hangs low in the sky during spring and autumn. I once spent a couple of days fishing under the smoke of a forest fire. It was odd: The air was orange, white ash fell all around, and the insects and fish rose into the never-ending twilight all day long.

COLD FRONT

The dreaded cold front almost always puts fish off—any fish, any-place. Just before a front hits in hot weather, especially in the autumn, however, the opposite occurs, often producing excellent fishing. Some nastiness associated with these systems, such as falling snow, can put trout on the feed. After the front pushes through the area, the fish usually sulk until the weather warms. If the water gets too cold, follow the weather carefully and fish a day or two after the temperature rebounds in late afternoon.

THUNDERSTORMS

For several years I guided on a ranch that featured a lodge overlooking a creek and a series of ponds. When not on the water, we would sit on the deck and scan the nearest pond for feeding trout. It was shallow, and the fish were surface oriented, so if no fish were rising, they weren't eating. In midsummer, it was common for thunderstorms to build midday, vent wind, rain, and lightning, and then move on. Over the course of several seasons, the trouts' feeding habits as storms blew through became clear from our observatory. Since then I have noticed the same tendencies during violent weather elsewhere.

When a thunderstorm was building, the fish were active, especially if there was cloud cover. When the wind started blowing, the feeding eased off. When the air really swirled, the fish would sulk. The lull usually lasted through the storm, but the trout would go back to feeding if the wind abated. The cloudy, humid calm after the storm was a very good time to fish.

CLOUDS

Cloud cover induces insect activity and consequently creates better fishing in general. Some very important insects—especially the blue-winged olive (BWO)—seldom hatch unless the weather is cloudy. Trout—and all animals—feel at ease under clouds and will venture out into the open.

RAIN

Trout love rain, and although fishing can be good in a downpour, it is almost always excellent in a light and steady drizzle—as long as there is little or no wind. The wind throws that unsettled component back into the equation and usually turns off the fish.

SUN, SHADE, AND SILHOUETTE

Experienced hunters instinctively use sun and shadow to their advantage. Predators naturally gravitate toward places where they have a lighting advantage over their prey. We fly fishermen don't need to function on that level of awareness, but we would catch and release more fish if we used light and shade to our advantage.

First and foremost, try to position the sun behind you in all fishing situations. You will have a better view of the fish, your fly, and the bottom. Of even greater importance is that the wary trout is less likely to see you when the sun is behind you. Conversely, when you are looking into the sun, the fish can see you, but you can't see it.

When approaching nervous fish, angle around until you can head in with the sun behind you. Don't blind yourself by looking up to figure out where the yellow ball is; just glance at your shadow and aim it toward the fish. Yes, like the old wives' tale says, your shadow cast over the fish would spook it, but this is only a concern when the sun is so low in the sky that your shadow is long.

Fishing with the sun in your favor is such a big factor in certain waters, such as small streams with slow pools, that I sometimes won't even bother fishing places where I am forced to fish with the sun in my eyes. Keep score of how you do with a low-slanting sun behind you and how you do with the sun in front of you. The results will prove the importance of keeping the light behind you whenever possible.

If you have the sun in your favor, you may be able to approach delicate water standing upright. If, however, the fish have a good chance of seeing you, get down. Trout can spook from a very long way off when you are highlighted against the sky, so look behind you and see if you are silhouetted. If you are, get down or utilize surrounding cover. Although anglers accustomed to fishing small streams are all too familiar with groveling on their knees to catch fish, many arrive upright and then get down. Start your approach with a walking crouch; gradually stoop lower and lower as you approach the water. That way your profile stays at the same height as you move into your final position.

On smaller streams, it is hard to catch more than one fish out of a tranquil pool under low-water conditions. If, however, you stay low

Stay close to cover whenever possible.

and don't stand up to land fish, the others might not spook and may be fooled as well.

Fishermen in the shade are much less likely to be spotted than those in the sun. The ideal setup is for the fish to be in the sunlight while you are lurking in the shadows. When the fish is in the shade and you are in the sun, it's "advantage—fish."

So, whenever possible, position yourself in the shadow of a tree, bush, or boulder. It is generally wise to stay close to such cover because standing in front of or next to a bush, regardless of the shadow factor, breaks up your silhouette.

If my clients are having poor luck fishing small mountain streams under favorable conditions, I always assume that the trout are getting spooked and resort to more stealth. A combination of planning the approach more carefully, keeping a low profile, and staying farther back does the trick.

A GUIDE'S ADVANTAGE

Guides get the jump on the best fishing. After years of experience in an area, guides know when to expect the conditions and hatches that produce the best fishing. So we start keeping a close eye on a particular piece of water. Then we are there to catch—and release—the fish when they are dumb and hungry.

7

Fishing Pressure

Any modern book about trout fishing in America has to cover fishing pressure and how to deal with the stressed breed of fish—and fishermen—that it produces. Catch-and-release has made for some wonderful sport, but many people make the erroneous assumption that released trout are easily captured again. Normally—except for a remote cutthroat perhaps—fish that have recently been molested become difficult to fool again; they just don't like being caught.

In the guiding business we think of fishing pressure as just one more factor that impacts the quality of fishing. It goes into the equation with other conditions. This is usually a short-term effect, as in, "Don't fish there 'cause Ol' Numb Nuts caught 'em all yesterday." (Ol' Numb Nuts is usually an unemployed local or off-duty guide.) But there is a general long-term effect as the season progresses, too. I recently suggested to one of my guides that we were too fond of a stretch of water and had added to the overall sophistication of the trout living there.

We have a couple of remote and private waters to which we have exclusive access. Knowing exactly how much the spot is fished, we can observe just how much fishing pressure it takes to make the trout shy—and it ain't much. Trout are as dumb as a box of rocks, and it is fishing pressure that makes them "smart." Last year I hiked into an extremely remote beaver pond to catch Rio Grande cutthroats. The biggest one was a beautiful 13-incher with a bright orange belly. I wanted a picture of it, but it unhooked itself and flopped off the bank and back into the water. I watched it slowly swim away. As an afterthought, I slapped the fly back on it when it was only feet away. To my amazement the beautiful creature slowly rose up and ate the fly again. After a lesser fight the fish came ashore again, and I got the photo.

Early-season trout and those that are seldom fished for will rise with abandon to gulp just about any fly, and unless they are in the midst of an intense hatch, such innocent creatures are not naturally selective. After we have harassed them, however, they become problematic and may even develop quirks. (The older a trout, of course, the hipper it is.) These quirks can vary from place to place; I know of one creek where the fish—cutthroats, no less—in reaction to fishing pressure have learned to spit flies out incredibly fast. Sometimes they become extremely spooky and highly selective. Heavy angling pressure can change their dining habits, too; trout (especially browns) learn that it is safer to eat subsurface and under low-light conditions.

On the fast-paced Madison River in Montana most of the prime water is along the edges—where the fish can get out of the current. But the high angling pressure forces them to occupy the faster water out farther. Consequently, a heavily weighted nymph fished in the river's main current is the most productive way to fish. If, however, you suspect that the piece of river you are fishing has not been trodden by anyone *yet that day*, fish the edges—stay low and quiet and cast from a distance. Being the first rod on busy water on any particular day is often well rewarded.

Famed San Juan guide Curtis Bailey works the "Juan" over three hundred days a year.

New Mexico's San Juan River has a tremendous number of big rainbows—nearly equaled by the number of fishermen pursuing them. Trout so besieged develop nervous habits, and the key to catching them is getting in tune with their quirks. Their little lunacies can be subtle, and you may be standing next to someone who is catching one right after the other, whereas you fish the same water in apparently the same manner with apparently the same fly and catch nothing. One day the trout are eating only No. 26 olive midge pupae presented just so, whereas the following day—or hour—they prefer a presentation and fly just a hair different. This gives you one big uphill climb if you are new on the block. Of course, in this type of situation a guide can make all the difference in the world, and if you can afford to hire one, it will pay off. The guide knows where and how to get into the *catchable* fish.

WOOLLY BUGGER 'EM

If you are without a guide, you may be able to even the playing field by "Woolly Buggering" them, as my son Nick calls it. When he is faced with temperamental, pain-in-the-ass fish, he doesn't stand there for hours scratching his head and picking through his fly box. Instead of being suckered in by an individual fish that may be nearly impossible to apprehend, Nick pounds the river with Woolly Buggers. By covering a lot of fish, he finds plenty of takers.

Actually, there are many times when you may do better by Woolly Buggering them than by matching the hatch. I remember one still and misty morning on a lake in southern Colorado when a huge midge hatch came off. The fish were rising everywhere, but I was having little luck getting any of them to see and take my minuscule imitation amongst the gazillion flies. I switched to a black Woolly Bugger, dragged it in front of those rising fish, and caught one after another. This is the modus operandi when going after fish that are not hounded.

OTHER ANGLERS ON SMALL STREAMS

Dealing with other anglers is a big problem on our crowded streams these days. Part of the problem may lie with differences in perspective. Folks from urban areas are used to being elbow to elbow and often volunteer their company with a smile—like it's the thing to do. Tension arises when these fishers encounter crusty hicks like me who secretly hate all "foreigners" encountered on "my water."

This animosity has validity on small creeks where the angler's greatest concern is spooking fish. If someone is fishing in front of you, you aren't going to catch anything. You should never fish behind another angler on small streams with wild trout if you can avoid it. To tell if there is someone fishing ahead of you, be on the lookout for water splashed up onto rocks. Tumbling water splashes water onto rocks, of course, but the clumsy feet of "foreigners" splash it even higher. It probably takes twenty to thirty minutes for those splashes to evaporate, which is about the same amount of time it takes spooked fish to return to feeding—albeit suspicious feeding.

If you see such signs of other anglers, don't continue fishing because the fish are likely to be spooked anyway. Instead, find the other angler and watch him for a couple of minutes to find out what he's up to. If, for instance, it's a beginner moving fast, you may want to relax a few minutes and let him fish on ahead. The neophyte only frightens the trout, and they may get back to near-normal after the crashing and splashing have stopped. You wouldn't, however, want to follow a really skilled angler. He will scour all the best water and hook many fish. Conversely, if the competition is moving slowly, you may want to go around and move up ahead. You certainly don't want to get into a jogging match from pool to pool; go far enough above him that he doesn't have to fish your tainted water.

It is a good policy to talk to the other person, but he may have thought he had the river all to himself and may resent your intrusion. But if you are planning to fish in front of him, having a little chat breaks the tension. (If you are "packin,'" be sure to show him your heat.) Maybe you can find out some pertinent information, such as where the other angler has been fishing, how he has fared, and so on. Ask if there are others in his party and where they are. Ask about his plans and then try to work out a simple arrangement that keeps everybody in good water.

No matter what your approach is to meeting others on little creeks, common sense and courtesy dictate that you leave anyone else plenty of elbow room. The amount of water will vary widely according to the degree of congestion. That may be just a couple of casts away, whereas in really remote places the appropriate distance between anglers could be a mile or more (surely if you are packin' heavy, you will get a long hunk of the best water). Dealing with other fishermen is part of trout fishing, and the more tactful your conduct, and the grander your pistola, the brighter the day.

BRING YOUR OWN ROCK

When I was doing fly-tying and -fishing schools with my old friend A. K. Best, he once told a group of students that he fished a place that was so busy that he had to "bring my own rock to stand on." A. K. is such a talented fisherman that he could catch fish in a bathtub, but how is Joe Average Fisherman going to get an edge when fishing-crowded water? (Without packing heat, that is.) I recently fished with a boyhood friend of mine at his house on the Batten Kill. Bill Luty is an excellent angler, and here are his findings.

High-pressure Observations

Bill Luty has fished fifty years on eastern rivers that have a lot of fishing pressure—and a lot of difficult, flat water. These rivers include the Farmington, Housatonic, Beaverkill, Willowemoc, New York's Ausable, Delaware, and his favorite, the Batten Kill. His observations will help an experienced fly fisher. Warning to beginners: Don't go here; it could be dangerous to one's sanity! Catching big trout even while surrounded by other fishermen.

Casting

Aim false casts away from a fish to eliminate water spray that can spook it. If possible, have the right length of line measured and gathered and shoot it out on the final stroke to reduce activity above a trout.

Noise

Bill says that the only time he has seen noise not be an issue on the Batten Kill is when fishing where trout are used to it, where the river runs alongside a factory that does metal forging ten hours a day—metal banging against metal all day long. Such fish are not noise conscious. (Bear in mind that shouting when you hook a fish is a no-no over flat water.)

Boaters and Floaters

Canoers, kayakers, rafters, and tubers are ever-present distractions on a well-used stream. Most are fisherman-friendly and will go around you if you ask them politely. Kayaks and canoes are okay if they are not banging paddles and hitting rocks. On the Housatonic and Farmington, fish will rise immediately behind a drift boat, canoe, or kayak after it quietly glides through. Tubers are another story. When they come through, you may want to ask them where they put in and are taking out so that you can go past there to avoid their commotion.

Other Fishermen

Don't expect a refined fisherman's etiquette in high-pressure rivers. Bill has seen fishermen slosh through a pool right in front of him while waiting for the fish to eat. And he's been sandwiched between two guys trying to force him out of a pool. The best thing to do in this instance is to nicely ask the people to go around you. It also helps to have alternate water to go to in high-pressure streams—water that many don't like to fish. This includes streams that are hard to wade, fast, or just outside the boundaries of the catch-and-release sections—or beyond where the trails stop.

Patience

In high-pressure water, take a spot and wait for the fish to rise. This claims your spot and gives the area a chance to recover before you cast. Most fishermen will honor that and not push unless invited. (Taylor Streit note: "Packing a sidearm" helps here.) On flat streams like the Batten Kill, if there are no fish rising when conditions are good, you are probably best off just to sit and wait for the fish to feed anyway.

Bad weather can produce big fish and fewer fishermen. This spring Bill fished the Batten Kill midweek with streamers during a dreary, drizzly rain and caught forty fish and never saw another angler.

THE RIGHT FLY CAN BE PARAMOUNT

Many times, of course, having the right fly is paramount, and we will address that in the next chapter, but after years of fishing and guiding, I bother less with trying to match the hatch—especially if the fish are big and the flies are small—because it is difficult to land heavy fish on tiny hooks and thin leaders. So if the trout aren't of the overly educated variety, and if they are feeding on No. 22 Trico nymphs, I usually have my client use a No. 16 short-shanked Beadhead Hare's Ear Nymph (or Shit Fly, Copper John, Pheasant Tail, et al.) on 4X tippet because that size hook and tippet will land large fish handily. In most streams the fish eat so many flies of that size and color that they just grab the little morsel as it goes by out of habit. Furthermore, the larger fly will be seen more easily by the fish than will the tiny, numerous Trico nymphs.

My son Nick recently told me an interesting anecdote. He was fishing the Clark's Fork in Montana and was having a hard time with the fish, even though he had been given the "right fly" by a friend of his who guides on the river. The fish, however, didn't seem to know that he was fishing the right fly and refused it. So he changed flies—again and again—until he wound up with the same fly with which he began, when he finally started catching fish. He deduced that he would have been better off to have kept putting the one recommended fly over the fish than to fuss with all those other flies.

When he told me this little story I started to think of the hundreds of times I've done the same thing. Selective trout can be like that; you just have to put your fly over them repeatedly, and maybe on the fiftieth pass they'll eat it. Incidentally, "over them" does not mean a foot or two away; practice your tip casting until you can aim that fly into the fish's mouth.

8

Hatches

It's great to be on the water during a good hatch, but I don't make that big a deal out of targeting specific hatches when guiding. Maybe that has to do with the nature of guiding. We don't say to the client, "The pale morning dun hatch starts at 11 a.m. and lasts for about an hour, so we can wrap it up by noon." No, we fish all day, through the good, the bad, and the ugly. What I'm really interested in is the general activity on the water throughout the day. If there is life abuzz and bugs in the air, the trout are far more likely to be feeding, whether or not they are eating a particular insect.

During multiple hatches some fish may feed on one insect, whereas others are partial to a different one. This is because certain insects are more available in particular portions of a stream and the fish that live in those places eat what's put on the table. For instance, caddis flies swarm near brush and crawl around streamside, so trout look for them there. Most mayflies, however, hatch in shallow riffles and then free-float mid-current. And end up in areas where surface debris is funneled.

The intensity of the hatch is also a factor because although you might see many small mayflies float by before the trout become interested in them, the sighting of one stonefly is enough evidence to tie on an imitation—because the largest trout in the river will have seen a lot more of them by then than you have and will be on the lookout for more.

On rare occasions there are too many natural insects, and the trout have too many choices. This is when you need to repeatedly put your fly right over the fish. Or use two flies here, one being an exact imitation of the insect and the other one being just a little different than the natural. Sometimes the fish will prefer the odd, or perhaps crippled, one. Also try the next-size-smaller fly if a fish won't take. (Do this during any hatch because the fly may look more realistic to the fish.) Lastly, use a fly that is different but not out of character with the stream, like a beetle (which is simply deadly for selective trout anywhere). Or when all else fails, try something really out there, like an orange Chernobyl Ant.

In our prerunoff caddis hatch on the Rio Grande it often works to use two dries, one of them being a very large yellow stonefly that really gets the fishes' attention. This works when the fish are way hungry and dumb.

TRICOS

This same principle can be used during Trico hatches. Give the fish something to draw their attention, like a hopper, when they are going crazy for the tiny—but all too numerous—Tricos.

But such stupid trout are unfortunately a rarity. Usually you have to be pretty careful about duplicating the stage of insect that is hatching at that exact time. And then place the fly directly over the fish to get them to eat it. After all, this is a very small meal—from size 18 to 24—and the trout aren't going to travel far to get one. This is a midsummer-to-fall event that is very underutilized. If you get hip to the timing, you can have great fishing every morning for over a month.

The bug goes through its complete life cycle in just a day. The males hatch at night, and the female duns come off early in the morning. So you need several different imitations in your pocket; during the dun hatch, use the dry with the upright white wings. (Later, when you switch to a fly that is hard to see, just tie it a foot in back of this visible one.) After the duns, the spinner fall occurs, and this is when the trout can slurp vast quantities of the dead insects. Use imitation of a dead Trico—something with spent-wings. (Spent-winged flies have wings that lie flat on the water.) These can be fished just below the surface, and there are also patterns that are designed to be fished subsurface. (The Hackle Stacker is a great fly here.) After the fish quit rising, continue to look in eddies and little nooks and crannies for more risers. The dead insects will be massed in these places after they have washed down the main flow.

BWOs

Another insect of great importance across North America is the blue-winged olive. This is another small mayfly (16 to 22) that fills a huge gap in the fly-fishing world because it hatches on the shoulder seasons of the year—early spring and late autumn—when little else might be available to eat. Trout rising to the adults are the main action, but fishing the nymph—an olive tungsten-head micro may in a size 18—is the ticket around hatch time when fish are not rising.

There are many intricacies to fishing and tying BWOs. I am not that well versed on them all and would refer the reader to other literature—A. K. Best's *A. K.'s Fly Box* is great for the serious fly tier. He is from Colorado, where there are many smart fishermen fishing for the smartest of trout. These guys use floating nymphs, submergers, floating emergers, woofers, tweeters, and so forth. A. K. gets very specific on this bug and suggested in our tying and fishing school that the wings for a certain size 16 imitation be size 17. And that the body for one species of the insect should be tied with fur the color of "faded split-pea soup."

Hendricksons, quill gordons, and similar blue dun and gray mayflies are important in many parts of the country. Here in the southern Rockies we usually encounter such hatches on summer evenings. The size range is from 12 to 16, with that middle size 14 being the most common. Years ago I happened to tie several dozen Gray Wulffs, and on the occasions when I run into such a hatch these rather crude flies—the body is tied with muskrat fur—have worked well because the trout don't seem all that particular when feeding on such mayflies. A Parachute Adams is—per usual—a good choice. In *A. K.'s Fly Box* he suggests using quill body patterns when more accurate imitations are required.

PALE MORNING DUNS

Different patterns of PMDs should be in everyone's dry-fly box. Old-style hackle imitations don't work as well as the Comparaduns and Parachutes. They should be from almost white or cream color to a shade that has a hint of olive and sometimes pink in it. Fishing the nymph of the insect is a good choice before the hatch begins. But when the hatch is on, the bright flies are numerous enough to get the fishes' attention. One of the good things about this hatch is that there are usually not so many insects that your fly is lost in a sea of them. Where I fish they should be called pale (late) morning dun, and often it is well into the far side of noon before we see them.

GREEN DRAKES AND FLAVILINEA

Where found, green drakes and "flavs" make trout dumber than a box of rocks. Of course, when they occur—in early summer—the fish are usually ignorant anyway and on the feed in general. These flies are big and just numerous enough to whet the trouts' appetite. The hungry fish will often swim several feet when sensing one nearby. These flies are encountered midday in our neck of the woods, often simultaneous with—but usually just after—the stonefly hatches.

The flav looks just like the green drake but is about a size 12. The proper green drake is much larger at a size 8 to 10. Be sure and have a few of the green drakes in your fly box because if you run into the hatch you are not going to have any other mayfly patterns close to it! And you don't want to miss out—it is a ten-day party!

Many patterns for the drake have extended bodies made of deer hair. Pick out ones without really long bodies for better hooking and get a handful because the deer hair is quickly trashed by a big trout's teeth. (The best pattern is Ben Furimsky's foam body drake—it floats like a cork and is a good choice if you have a nymph below.)

STONEFLIES

There are several types of stoneflies, but generally the larger they are, the more important the subspecies. If you're a fish, consuming a big salmon fly is like eating about fifty normal-size bugs, and the trout respond accordingly. Just seeing one in the air or on a branch should inspire you to tie one on. The dark-colored nymphs of the giant stones will be found under larger rocks close to the bank when the flies are about to hatch. When the hatch gets going—in June when rivers are still in runoff—the bugs will fly about noon. Imitations with orange bodies are the norm. Trout are so fond of this insect that they seem to remember them, and I will often use a big stone as my first fly in a dry/dropper rig all summer.

GOLDEN STONES

These stoneflies do not get the respect from the trout that giant stones do in my area because they hatch rather sparingly. But I know that they are more important in northern portions of the Rockies. They hatch a little later in summer than do the giant stones.

YELLOW SALLIES

These light green stoneflies hatch in midsummer. Smallish and demure (size 12 to 14), they tend to blend into the grass where they light. But they are a preferred trout food. The fly pattern should be slim and sparse in appearance but with a white post for visibility. They hatch on still midsummer days when little seems to be happening.

CADDIS FLIES

Fishing encounters with caddis can range from being bombarded by blizzards of 'em in early spring to having sporadic brushes with smaller specimens on quiet summer evenings. They are a prolific insect, and

When insects are thick—like during the caddis hatch—try and get to the event early, before the fish become jaded.

the encased larvae will be found under every rock in a large stream. The green rock worm is the most common. It builds a cocoon of tiny rocks around itself and hatches prerunoff (April–May). This hatch can last a couple of weeks, but turbulent weather and water conditions common to that time of year often stall or terminate the event. Trout can put on massive amounts of weight during the hatch. On some afternoons and evenings the flies can be so numerous that the trout never bother to rise, preferring to eat the drifting pupae only. A wet imitation of a pupa can then be swung on the current. As the fly is raised to the surface, the trout grab it. (We called this the Leisenring lift back in the day.)

Skating flies is a great way to draw attention to your fly when it is in the midst of thousands of others. When the big caddis hatch hits in early spring, it can be windy, and if there is much bank structure the insects will swarm in the lees behind rocks, river bends, and trees.

Many varieties of caddis will also be found along brushy stream banks throughout the warmer months. But these tend to be smaller, making a size 16 Elk Hair Caddis one of the best "go-to" dry flies on Planet Trout. If you tie and want the perfect Elk Hair Caddis, find very light-colored, short elk hair from the flank of an early season elk. (It should have a faint understory that is almost furlike.) Tie the wing with it because it is durable, buoyant, and bright. Bleached coastal deer is an acceptable choice otherwise.

CALLIBAETIS AND DAMSELFLIES

Callibaetis are lake mayflies that have a brown speckled wing and hatch midmorning in summer. They are usually a size 14 to 16. Fish do not seem to be overly selective when they are feeding on them, and a Parachute Adams is fine. But wind will blow them off the lake. A rise to them will be a rather normal swirl, whereas a rise to a mature damselfly will often be a leaping affair. To differentiate is important because both bugs are often found hatching about the same time of day. The adult damsels are usually bright blue and are most common where sticks or grass protrude from the water. The insects land on this structure and trout will be found cruising close by waiting to snatch one, so lay your fly nearby and wait.

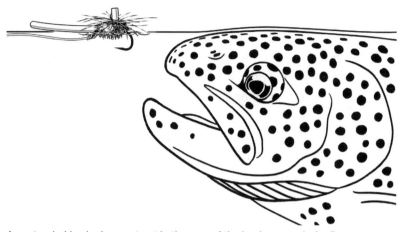

An extended body does not get in the way of the business end of a fly.

Most adult damselfly imitations have extended bodies, but bodies that extend past the bend of the hook will hook fish poorly. That's because the extended portion is first encountered by the fish's mouth, and the hook point is thus pushed away. If the trout gets hooked, it is usually just barely hooked. My Fly Line Damsel has an extended body but extends *over the eye,* leaving the business section of the hook exposed.

The damsel nymph is available to the trout in shallow water much of the time. It is usually a pastel olive or beige and swims with an undulating motion. Gary Borger in his book *Designing Trout Flies* suggests retrieving this fly by shaking the rod tip back and forth to simulate the motion this nymph makes. Gary has done a lot of good work on lake fishing and so may be onto something, but a regular retrieve works about as well for me and is less work. The damselfly nymph should be tied on a regular-length hook with an extended marabou body to simulate its hula dance; it is the "go-to" fly for many lake-fishing situations. Note: An extended *soft* body does not reduce hookups.

MIDGES

Making up a huge portion of trout diets, midges in many waters are *all* there is to eat. This is true not only on famous tailwaters but also in many still waters. And they must be quite delicious because trout will target them, and the largest fish will hunt for midges in the shallowest of waters. Midges hatch at different times of the day but mostly in evenings. But there seem to be hatches of them in different parts of a lake *at different times of the day.* You can often find areas where trout are rising by scanning with binoculars. Little or no wind is necessary so you can see the rises.

My way of fishing midges in lakes is often to just cover a lot of fish with larger flies, and a certain percentage of them will eat a Woolly Bugger—or some such juicy fly. But this doesn't work on trout that have been fished to a lot, nor does it work on tailwater fish that feed almost exclusively on midges.

Some of the best info on lake fishing midges is in Craig Mathews's book *Western Fly-Fishing Strategies.* One important observation he makes about fishing for trout actively rising to midges is to "never make a presentation to a riser more than 50 feet away. . . . Be patient and hold your fire until a fish gets closer and your presentation can be properly made."

TIMING COUNTS

The timing of hatches should be considered, too. Too bad all aquatic insect hatches aren't as predictable and dependable as the pale morning dun or BWO hatches. On a day-to-day basis, however, hatches are predictable on a given river as long as conditions stay the same. If conditions change, adjustments can be made. For example, if the blue-winged olives normally start at 3 p.m., and a cold front moves into the area, the insects will most likely come off later in the day. Such hatches create the scenario that results in really good fishing. In reality, many hatches are encountered by chance, and by the time you find the right fly, the party is already over. If you know when it's going to happen, you can not only have the right imitation on but also be waiting at the right place at the right time.

9

"Strike!"

I was recently in Taos Fly Shop—in Taos, New Mexico, of course—talking to shop manager and guide Daniel Gentle. Seems that the day before Danny had a client who knew his entomology and had all the right gear but couldn't hook any fish. Dan, being the astute guide that he is, stood back a few paces and tried to see if he could figure out the problem.

SET THE HOOK

From a distance he could see that when the man set the hook, his arm sprang straight up, but his rod stayed horizontal to the water. It was the dreaded "strike that ain't." This is a rather common problem and is perhaps a nervous reaction to facing the moment of truth. I've seen excitable clients jump straight up into the air at the sight of the fish taking the fly but never actually set the hook. The "strike that ain't" is a similar response.

Too much attention is paid to obscure and overrated aspects of fly fishing: leader formulas, persnickety fly design, and subspecies of insects—the list is endless. Little, if anything, however, is ever mentioned about that instant action of utmost importance: setting the hook. After seeing thousands of fish missed because of late and faulty striking, I can assure you that this overlooked aspect of fly fishing gets absolute top billing with me.

If you are going to hang on to a fish, the hook must be set. On hard-mouthed fish like tarpon this is a huge aspect. By contrast, we tend to think that the setting of a hook in a wee trout isn't important, but if you tend to lose fish after they have been on for just a short time, it is likely that the hook point wasn't driven home in the first place. Hold a hook against your skin and imagine how much pressure it would take to bury it. It would be quite a bit. If you think you may not have sunk the fly

The dreaded "strike that ain't." The arm goes up, but the rod stays horizontal—the line never draws tight.

into the fish's mouth when you initially struck, set the hook again while fighting the fish. Incidentally, a hook penetrates easier if the barb has been removed.

USE ENOUGH TIPPET

Of course, use a tippet heavy enough to match the job. You can't really set a No. 6 Woolly Bugger with 6X tippet, although a lot of people try. I often guide beginners who invariably have several spools of terribly thin tippet. The neophyte, as well as the clerk who sold him the stuff, believes that trout are such clever creatures that anglers had better play it safe and use only 6X. The truth is that such frail line is seldom prudent and that people can usually use much heavier tippets than they do. An exception would be certain tailwaters and spring creeks, where the flies are tiny and the fishing pressure is great. I use 3X and 4X for most of my fishing. I believe 5X is for flies under No. 18, and 2X is usually okay for streamers.

(Fluorocarbon is much stronger than regular mono, so adjust accordingly—and go one size thinner when using it.)

DETECTING THE BITE

You have more time to set the hook on a big fish than on a small one. It simply takes longer for a fly to travel in and out of a bucket mouth. And when the hook is set into a large fish, it is being driven into something solid that doesn't give. So your terminal tackle sets—and breaks—easily. Small trout, on the other hand, may simply be pulled toward you when the hook set is attempted, and they are never actually hooked.

If every nymph fisherman knew how many undetected and missed strikes he had in the course of a day, it would change the way he fished forever. Whenever possible, I take up a position well above the stream so that I can spot fish for my client. When the fisherman is casting a nymph to an individual fish, I have found it is better for me to watch the fish rather than the indicator. When I assume the fly is in the neighborhood of the trout, I look for the fish to move or open its mouth. I then screech, "Strike!" at the top of my lungs.

This is by no means foolproof because the fish may not be eating the nymph. Instead, it might be just yawning, but results over the years have proven it is better for me to watch the fish than the indicator because very often the indicator never moves when the trout eats the fly.

Most fly fishermen have the notion that trout take food in various fashions. The moody rascals "nail it" sometimes and "take it real gently" at other times. It's true that when they are very hungry or chasing moving prey, they take assertively—and on those occasions they are easier to hook. Conversely, when they are not so hungry, they tend to pick and nibble and are more difficult to latch onto. Because most of the food trout eat is free-floating and can't escape, however, fish usually inhale their meals rather leisurely, often drifting along with the fly as they eat it. Such a take causes no hesitation in the path of the strike indicator. Nor will the indicator react when a fish comes toward you to take the fly.

Think of the lazy trout eating like you do. He casually picks up a bug like you would a hamburger—it's not going anywhere. If the meal is about to get away, however, and is passing behind the trout in fast water, the fish may rush to get it before it washes away. (If your Big Mac slips out of your hands, you'll make a stab for it before it hits the floor.) Such a fish will be easy to hook because the indicator will race upstream as the animal heads back to its feeding station. The fly will probably not be ejected until the fish gets back there. Remember, however, that more often than not, a trout nonchalantly takes a fly that is passing next to it. Its little, uncluttered brain will notice that there is a hunk of metal hanging off the proposed meal, and he will eject the phony immediately, giving you only a fraction of a second to react.

To illustrate this point, I once had a client who wanted to go beyond catch-and-release—to strike-and-release—so we cut the hook off right at the bend. We were fishing for cutthroats in a stream that is heavily fished, and those trout, after the first week or two of the season, spit the fly out incredibly fast. Those same trout grabbed the hookless fly and swam around the creek with it like a dog with a bone.

RECOGNIZE AND REACT

Undoubtedly the two most costly mistakes that nymph fishermen make are not recognizing a take and then not striking fast enough. This is especially true for beginning anglers who have not developed a level of concentration that is equal to the task. It is also true even for experienced fly fishers when they are not on their game. I know that when I'm tired I miss a lot of strikes. The indicator makes a slight jiggle; the event tours the foggy mind, and a decision is finally made to set the hook.

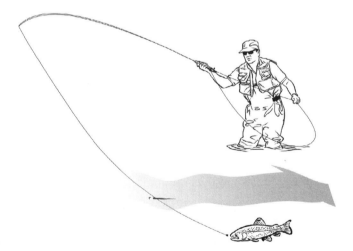

This striking motion is poor because it pulls the fly out of the fish's mouth.

Too late! The secret is to concentrate, and then, when anything "funny" happens, to shoot first and ask questions later. Set that hook now! It is better to strike too fast and hard and break fish off now and then than to be too slow and miss them all. Take your nymph out of the water with enough authority to set the hook—don't lift the rod slightly to see if you have a "nibble."

When you are upstream nymph fishing in deep water, the most likely place you'll get a strike may be right beside or below you. This is where the fly is running the deepest and is the most effective. In this situation your rod should be moving at the same pace as your fly and downstream of it. The drift should be extended as far as possible by reaching below you. Unfortunately most anglers blow it when they get a strike from that position because they set the hook with the standard upward lift of the rod. That motion pulls the fly in the wrong direction—out of the fish's mouth. Furthermore, this upward motion slows contact because it changes the angle of the rod, forming slack between the rod tip and the fly. If the strike is made downstream, however, with a motion that is a continuation of the rod's downstream movement, you'll get the quickest contact between rod tip and fly.

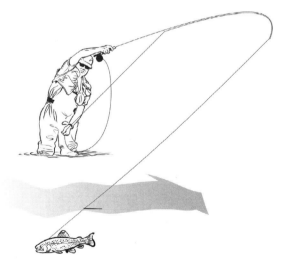

This is an efficient striking motion. The hook makes faster contact with the fish, and the angle promotes better hook penetration.

When trout take a dry fly, they rise up to eat it and don't eject it until they return to their feeding station. The best time to set the hook is when the fish is heading downward. Consequently, a somewhat leisurely strike is best. If the dry is small—under No. 18—set the hook gently, especially if you are using a stiff rod, so the tiny gap doesn't rip through the fish's flesh.

SIGHT-FISHING CHALLENGE

Sight fishing for big trout with dries is high drama. Because these bruisers rise in an unhurried manner, they give you plenty of time to get overamped, and it is really easy to set the hook too soon and too hard, when the fish's mouth is still open and facing upward. Wait for the jaws to close and then set the hook.

As Dave Ames notes in his book, *A Good Life Wasted,* slack is evil. There is no way this angler can pull everything tight and hook this fish.

DON'T "SLACK" OFF

Most anglers are lazy about controlling their slack line and would hook a lot more fish if they were more aggressive about taking it up. They often cease recovering line toward the end of the drift and wind up with the rod pointing skyward and slack at their feet. This makes it physically impossible for them to pull the line tight and set the hook if a fish should take in close quarters.

DRY FLY–NYMPH COMBO

The dry fly with a beadhead dropper below it is murder on trout, and if you can set the nymph quickly and the dry slowly, you will catch even more on this setup.

THE "LET-'EM-TAKE-IT" STRIKE

I used to miss a lot of trout when retrieving a fly. Then I trolled a lake alone in a rowboat and learned the "let-'em-take-it" strike. I discovered that when I was rowing and the rod was propped up in the stern and out of my hands I caught more fish than when I was holding the rod. When I had the rod in my hands I would set the hook at every little bump, but when manning the oars I couldn't respond to those "nibbles," and that allowed the fish to take the fly. Since then I have watched many trout follow retrieved flies. They often nip and tuck at them, especially Woolly Buggers, before they take. If you set the hook during one of those pecks, you are simply pulling the fly out of his sight. If you do miss a fish like that, cast back to it immediately.

So when swinging, retrieving, or trolling a fly, resist the natural urge to strike and wait until you feel the weight of the fish before setting the hook. Don't raise the rod to set the hook but use a strip strike. That way the fly does not get taken out of the fish's zone if it is missed, and the fish has the chance to grab it again. To have great success with the strip strike, retrieve with long, even sweeps. When you feel a fish, just keep the motion going with the retrieving hand. When the weight of the fish is indeed a reality, *then* raise the rod while keeping the finger tight on the line.

Finishing a retrieve so that you can make a curved-line strike really boosts hookup percentages. When the fly is fairly close, perhaps 20 feet

Seventeen pound rainbow hooked by means of "strip strike" from Jurassic Lake Argentina. *Nick Streit*

away from you, raise the rod to complete the retrieve. Do this slowly and evenly so that the line gets a belly in it, and watch for that belly to tighten as the fly approaches you. If you see the line start to straighten, set the hook. When a fish grabs the fly on a slack line like that, hookup percentages soar. Unfortunately, fish can take flies very deep this way and may become gill hooked.

This is a good hooking technique when you are fishing sinking lines in lakes because trout often follow the fly. If you lift the rod slowly, they have a chance to take it. Experience has taught me to not just rip a fly out of the water when it is well below the surface but rather to swim it all the way to the top so that a following fish has a chance to get it.

SHORT AND TIGHT

Some fly fishers inadvertently let line slide under their finger when they set the hook. If you are missing a lot of strikes—or fish come off after a short time—make sure you have the line clamped down under your finger when you set the hook.

A LITTLE GIVE

But if it is a heavy trout, you have to instantly back off so that the fish doesn't break off. This is an extremely common happening at the lake we fish—Eagle Nest Lake in northern New Mexico. The trout are very healthy and heavy and can be expected to snap off inexperienced anglers almost half the time when they are fishing a retrieved fly—even with 3X fluorocarbon. (My son Nick has his clients use 0X!)

To give a little, let slack line ease from under your finger instantly after hooking the fish. If you are not sufficiently dexterous with the hands to do this, lower the rod or even run toward the fish if the water isn't deep.

GET CLOSE

Whenever you have a choice, especially when nymph fishing, fish a short line because it's hard to hook fish consistently when there is a lot of line on the water. Perhaps all the stretch in a long length of fly line is part of the problem. Trout can spit flies out so quickly that I wonder if the speed of light doesn't come into play here because like those stars that blow up "way out there," by the time we see it, it's already happened.

10

Catch My Drift

The concept of dead-drifting a dry fly or nymph is really very simple: The fly has to sail along in the current like a natural insect does—free floating. This sounds easy, but doing it when the fly is attached to a leader is not. It would be a snap if all rivers flowed at an even pace from bank to bank, but if that were the case, trout fishing would be a dull game. Outwitting weaving currents keeps it interesting.

Using long, thin tippets helps a fly act naturally, but long leaders are unwieldy, inaccurate to cast, and easy to break. They certainly aren't a cure-all for fooling trout. What usually gets you the best drift is having the line, leader, and fly all in the same current. Casting cross-stream subjects your line and leader to different currents, so fishing as straight upstream as possible is normally the best means to get a good drift. You can do several things to get the best float when fishing upstream: having proper positioning, reaching, reach casting, high sticking, refloating, and mending. And sometimes the best fisherman will be seen walking beside a fly that is drifting well in order to extend the length of that drift.

PROPER POSITIONING

Getting into proper position is the most desirable option because it presents the simplest and most straightforward solution. Aggressive wading becomes important here because getting into the ideal position can be difficult. After guiding thousands of people I have come to the conclusion that more fish will be caught if the angler gets close. Yes, a fish will be spooked here and there, but closer is almost always better. I'm forever begging my clients to "wade out just a step farther." The position you seek would allow you to place your fly straight upstream and just a little to your right if you are right-handed, to the left if you are a southpaw. From that position, your fly, strike indicator, leader, and line are all in

Point your rod tip at the fly as it drifts.

the same speed of current. As they drift downstream toward your rod tip, which is to your right, the rod should be pointed at the fly. When the fly gets within 25 feet, raise the rod to take up the remaining slack. That way you don't have to take up all the slack by hand, and when the rod becomes vertical you will be in position to make the next cast, with enough line out of the rod so that it loads easily. Just as they do when "high sticking," anglers tend to lift the rod too soon, that is, when they have too much line on the water.

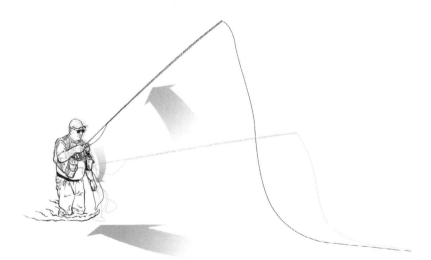

Toward the end of the drift—when the fly is within 20 feet—slowly pick up slack by raising the rod.

Raising the rod prematurely not only causes the fly to drag but also can create excess slack between rod tip and fly. As previously stated, if there is slack and the rod is in a vertical position, it is impossible to tighten the line and set the hook.

REACHING

Unfortunately, ideal positioning is seldom easy to obtain. Rivers are often too deep, fast, and wide for you to get where you need to be, in which case the next-best option is getting as close as you can to that position and "reaching." Reaching is the solution when there is a current of a different speed between you and your fly, but you have to be close enough to that current so that you can lift the line out of the flow. The longer the rod in this situation, the better. By raising the rod *horizontally,* you can lift the line off the water, reposition it elsewhere, and even add a mend at the same time.

REACH CAST

A reach can be applied when a cast is being laid down and is sensibly called the reach cast. It is a little tricky to perform because the reach needs to be applied as the line is falling to the water. Consequently, the cast needs to be deadened to allow time for the rod to be maneuvered right or left during the line's descent.

HIGH STICKING

Even though the term *high sticking* sounds more appropriate in a sports bar, it is an accurate description of a fly-fishing maneuver. It is really just reaching out with the extended arm to lift the line and leader off the water and follow it downstream. Remember that this maneuver is for short lines only. Anglers get too fond of high sticking and often try it when their fly is too far away. Furthermore, few people make full use of their arm the way they could. The appendage can be extended to make that 9-foot rod a longer and better tool, but instead the arm usually hangs limp at the angler's side. As much as I hate to cast aspersions, my observations lead me to conclude that the average fly fisher is a lazy cuss.

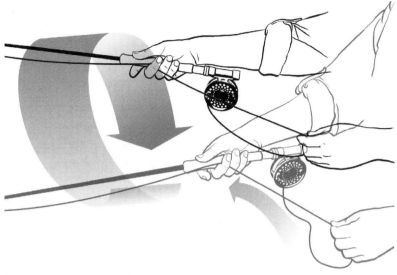

Mend only when necessary.

MENDING

Many situations may call for "mending." Used indiscriminately, the technique can be detrimental. If a fish decides to take just as a mend is being performed, the angler will invariably miss the strike because the hands and mind are busy. People get into the habit of mending because they fish a particular river where it is necessary to mend. On some waters, guides have their clients throw mends on each cast. Because it's a good idea for some rivers, however, doesn't mean it's a good idea else-where. The worst offense is the obligatory mend that is thrown just after the fly lands. (Tailwater and eastern fly fishers are prone to this.) This is often the exact time a fish jumps onto a fly, and by tossing a superflu-ous mend, the angler may either pull the fly out of the action or put the hands out of position to set the hook. I hesitate to show clients how to mend because they often become enamored with throwing those cute little loops and then start flipping the line all over the place! Use the operation only when necessary.

A mend is accomplished by pointing the rod at the fly, lifting the rod a little to get the line off the water, and then, in the same motion, rotating the wrist in the direction you want the line to go. If the motion has the proper snap to it, it will force the rod tip into a quick little roll that will be transmitted down the fly line, forcing a loop of line to hop off the water. If you want to make a bigger loop, make the motion bigger and slower. If you are a beginner and have never done this, you'll find it is easier to execute than I have made it sound. The trick is to perform the mend without affecting the drift of the fly. But don't panic if the fly gets jostled; even the best anglers do that. Some rods mend better than others, and thinner fly lines are easier to mend than thicker ones.

When fishing upstream, take up slack at a pace fast enough that the fly line doesn't loop below the rod tip. Most anglers are much too lax about slack line. When it gets excessive, drag is increased, and strikes are missed. In really fast water it is a lot of work to keep ahead of charging line. You can stay ahead in the race by pulling in long sweeps, starting as soon as the fly hits the water. Many anglers' strips are too short and jerky, and that doesn't get the job done. Make the first and all subsequent sweeps long and smooth.

When you are fishing upstream into a pool that spills out very quickly at the tail, try to be close enough for your rod tip to reach over

Whenever possible, have your rod tip over the water you are fishing so that the current can't grab the line.

If this angler were to move to his right, the line would lie on rock (x) and not be sucked out of the pool. *Wes Edling*

the pool itself. If you are too far back, the line catches in the fast current that's breaking over the lip of the pool; it will grab the line and drag the fly. It may be impossible to get close enough to get into ideal position, but you may be able to lay your line over a rock to keep it from dragging. By moving a step to your right or left, you can have your line fall onto a rock, where the current can't get hold of it.

Although a mend is often a good idea at the very end of a float, just before a fly is going to drag, reaching way out with the rod is a better choice. You avoid a difficult mend, and you're in a much better position to set the hook should your fly be attacked.

11

Flies

Because I've been "forced" to tie thousands of flies to earn a living, I have great respect for the art exhibited in a finely tied fly—but I must also confess that years on the water have left me a nonbeliever concerning the "mystique" surrounding fly patterns. On countless occasions a companion and I have fished in different directions, and at the end of the day we found that we had about the same amount of luck but on totally different flies. When you're in the thick of catching fish you'd swear that the fly is the secret of your success; more likely, the fish simply started feeding when you attached Mr. Lucky Fly to the leader.

Mr. Lucky is then his owner's favorite fly—until it is dethroned by another pattern that finds its way onto the leader on another fortuitous

Can changing flies make a difference? Sometimes—although if the fish aren't feeding, they aren't feeding.

occasion. Personally, I've had a hundred "favorite flies" that have gone in and out of fashion.

Almost every fly fisher I've ever met is under the illusion that changing flies will make the fish eat. My clients are forever saying, "Why don't we try something different?" I, too, always hope that the next fly is going to do it, though my experience would have me say, "No sense changing flies because the fish aren't feeding."

CHOOSING THE RIGHT DRY FLY

Admittedly my simplistic approach to fly choice is in part due to the fact that I usually fish for stupid trout in relatively remote areas. When trout are hounded and/or are feeding on a particular food, they may require considerable head scratching. But choosing the right fly is not really that complicated. For instance, a Parachute Adams in an appropriate size will imitate almost all mayflies, and by changing to another body color, it would imitate all mayflies.

Although I was raised fishing the famous Catskill dry flies like Quill Gordons and Light Cahills, these hackled, high-riding flies just don't produce like Parachutes and Comparaduns because those flies ride with their bodies flush on the water like a natural. The Comparadun style of fly was created out of the Haystack, of which I tied thousands when I was a teenager. That was on the Ausable River in New York, working for the late Fran Betters.

On flat water and in good light it is easy for the fish to examine a dry, so a Comparadun presents a realistic silhouette. When I'm tying dries I check the all-important silhouette by holding the fly above me at arm's length, toward the sky, and then examine it with squinted eyes. This is not a highly scientific approach and might be based on a wrong assumption, but this is how I suspect a trout sees a fly. A dry that imitates a mayfly should have a thin body that tapers from thick toward the eye to thin by the tail.

With a caddis the body should be tapered in the other direction, but, more importantly, a caddis's wing needs to be tent style over the body. Hoppers have a similar profile, but many commercial grasshopper patterns are tied out of proportion. A natural grasshopper is a fat bug, and many hopper imitations are simply too skinny.

SEEING IS BELIEVING

The first rule of thumb with dries is this: Whenever possible, use flies you can see. That means they have to float well because if they sink, you can't see them. So when there are no flies on the water to guide your choice, start with the big, bright, and bushy. If fish come up for your large dry and make splashy rises, but you feel nothing when you set the hook, you are getting false strikes. False strikes occur when the trout changes its mind at the last second and its tail slaps the surface as it heads for home. When that happens, a smaller version of the same fly often does the trick. Which size dry you choose also depends on the time of the season. Insects tend to be larger and trout dumber and hungrier at the beginning of the season.

A large Royal Stimulator (size 6 or 8) is my favorite fly dry when using a dry/dropper setup. (That's how I fish and guide 90 percent of the time.) It floats like a cork because, besides being hackled in front and having a palmered body, the fly has two buoyant wing materials (deer and calf tail), and if one substance decides to sink, the other often floats. If it does sink, it often "refloats" itself, and few flies do that. But remember that, if it goes under, a fish is most likely chewing on the nymph—and it's not "a rock," as my clients are destined to say.

EMERGERS

A trout that is truly rising for floating flies will stick its head above water occasionally, but many fish that you think are rising are in fact feeding just below the surface on emergers (insects that are struggling to hatch). When these fish first start feeding they might take a dry, and as a hatch progresses they will likely switch to eating flies off the surface, but if the fish you are up against refuses your dry after two or three drifts, give it an emerger just below the surface.

EASY-TO-TIE, EFFECTIVE-TO-USE NYMPH

I might get run out of town for confessing this, but I fish one nymph pattern 80 percent of the time. My "favorite fly" is an ugly rascal but very easy to tie. It was born of noble birth as a full-fledged Beadhead Gold-Ribbed Hare's Ear Nymph. But I have reduced it to such an extent that I hate to embarrass the famous pattern by continuing to call it by its given name. Actually I can't take credit for the development of this fly—the "reductions" were the fishes' doing—or should I say their undoing. Because they were so fond of the original, their enthusiasm stripped it of its tail and hackle. If the fish were going to amputate those appendages and continue to attack the fly at the same lustful rate, I told myself, why should I bother tying all the stuff on in the first place? Then the gold ribbing got ensnarled in some of the trouts' teeth, and the fly still caught fish. So it seemed to me that that accoutrement could be deleted as well. What that leaves is some brown fur with a gold bead ahead of it. Smear it with superglue and, voila, the Shit Fly. I suspect that the fly could even go a step further—just gold bead on a hook without any help from the fur behind, but I'm not ready to be that blasphemous—just yet.

I tie them on short-shanked, wide-gap hooks because I then have a fly that imitates a No. 18 but has the gap of a 16. Because I like being able to just change flies instead of adding or subtracting weight, I tie them in a couple of different-size beads.

I suspect that we humans are pretty limited in how we "see" flies. Because basically that's about it—we "see" the fly only visually. But fish can hear, smell, and feel vibrations. And there may be more things that affect a fly that may not fit into our realm of comprehension. I came up with a fly—the Poundmeister—that took years to get right, mostly because I was thinking only visually. It imitates a crane fly larva, an important fly to imitate because it is targeted by big trout early in the season and is a large and meaty insect. (It is especially common in low-elevation silted waters.) Originally I tied it with my favorite fish-catchin' materials: peacock, fur, and flash. But it didn't fish all that well until I palmered it with dun hackle; I speculate that the performance improved because the hackle suspends the fly in the current like a natural crane fly larva—tied without the hackle it just sinks straight away like a spent torpedo.

This fly has caught trout from Alaska to Argentina. It is a great first choice where big trout live because they prefer such substantial and defenseless entrées. Tied on a size 6–8 hook, the fly can accommodate a large bead, and that gets it down deep. (This insect can be very large, but I no longer use the really big versions because that size of fly is resistant to both casting and sinking.) The generous size also allows it to be tied on a heavy tippet, and this helps land large fish—as does the wide-gapped hook—which holds in a fish's mouth for the long period required to tire a heavy trout.

Beadhead Poundmeister (photo page 24)
Hook: Dar-Riki #135, sizes 4–8 (scud hook)
Thread: 3/0—gray
Bead: 3.80 millimeter or 4.5 millimeter—build up thread behind bead and then superglue (superglue entire shank)
Body:
1. Wide gray or pale olive chenille
2. Beaver fur over the chenille
3. Rib with blue dun hackle
4. Ten strands of peacock over the top—do not trim
5. Rib with copper wire
Head: wind peacock behind bead and superglue

THE PLUS AND MINUS OF STREAMERS

Unless my clients are after only big fish—or there's a great deal of water that can be fished (floated)—I seldom have them use streamers. They are an exciting type of fly to use because many fish are seen as they chase them. The problem is that often not that many of the trout actually take streamers (we joke about the guys who come into the shop and tell us how many fish they "moved"—much like "jumping" tarpon). They are great flies for locating big trout. When guiding a few times I have put a nymph on a big trout when it threatens a streamer but doesn't take. The fish may not be fooled by the streamer, but it may have inspired his appetite enough that he gloms the nymph.

I have noticed that most anglers want to fish streamers that are too small. Fish of decent size are attracted to big food.

Last summer my son Nick and I were fishing a remote stream in the southern Rockies. We were trading off fishing the creek and catching the ignorant browns at a brisk pace. When it was my turn to fish the next

Gabe Fontanazza on Chimehuin River, Argentina. When choosing a streamer, remember that big fish prefer big meals.

pool I hooked a 9-inch trout that got relocated at my all-too-vigorous strike. It came off the hook when it landed, yet a half-second later it started jumping all over the place. Then Nick and I saw, to our amazement, a trout that was maybe 18 inches grab the 9-incher. It was like watching a snake eating something that is too big for it. The bigger fish became totally incapacitated by trying to swallow such a hearty meal. As they tumbled downriver we followed as the larger fish continued to consume the smaller. By the time they had drifted 50 yards downstream, all that was left of the 9-incher was the tail sticking out the mouth of the bigger brown.

In Argentina I once had a brown trout of about 10 pounds rush up and grab a 12-inch rainbow that I was in the process of landing. Big fish want big meals, and our streamers are too small. I just measured the biggest streamer in my fly box, and it was 2 inches long—just an appetizer for a grown-up brown trout.

For good information on fishing streamers, check out Kelly Galloup's videos.

OUTSIDE THE "FLY" BOX

Some of the best patterns aren't really "flies" at all.

Because the trout season in the Rocky Mountain states is year-round, we fish where and when trout are spawning. The average fisherman's rod is hung on the wall at spawning time, so many anglers don't know much about the subject. And many other anglers have ethical and esoteric questions about fishing with egg patterns. Understandable because these "flies" work so well that it can feel like cheating. And they, of course, work best when trout are spawning. And trout have an eye out for the eggs then because there is usually little insect activity during spawning time.

In our area we use a light orange soft egg—sometimes with a red dot. A beadhead usually improves the fly and gets it down where it belongs—and the bright bead further draws the fish's attention. A fun part of egg fishing is that it is often possible to sight fish with the submerged fly—it is an admittedly rare occurrence to see both fly and the fish. But trout will sometimes travel 10 feet to glom a bright egg. In water that is getting fished a lot, the egg may draw their attention but then be refused. In such a situation tie a small, realistic nymph 2 feet behind the egg.

In Alaska they use a hard plastic egg that slides on the leader. When the fish takes, a gentle reaction pulls a circle hook into the corner of the mouth.

In springtime trout may congregate below other spawning fish, such as suckers, and eat their roe. Sucker eggs are beige in color and wash down in clumps. Big trout learn to key on such events and will gain much weight during a sucker egg "hatch."

Worms are big and meaty and squiggle as they go down—and fishermen have known that fish love to eat them for years. The San Juan Worm was a "fly" originated in the 1970s by the late Jim Aubrey and Bob Pelzl of Albuquerque. It was tied to imitate an aquatic worm on its namesake river but since then has been fished worldwide and tied in various colors and forms. We fish it a lot, but I believe that it imitates regular earthworms in our area because it works wonders in the spring when water is high and dirty and earthworms are available. Being born a bait fisher, I used to fish live earthworms on such occasions and know they should be fished deep and on a dead drift like a nymph. (Worms squiggle, but they don't swim.)

And—being born a bait fisher—I can't resist killing one trout for fillets each spring when the flesh is pink and cold. This year the 4-pound rainbow I extracted from a local lake had its stomach crammed full of earthworms. The water had been rising rapidly and had inundated the shallows; the fish were in just a foot of water and eating earthworms as they were forced out of the earth by the rising lake level.

12

Nymphs

As emphasized in Chapter 9 ("Strike!"), anglers detect only a portion of their nymph strikes and then hook only a fraction of those fish. The quickest will hook 50 percent at best. Consequently, a nymph needs to be rigged and fished so that it not only attracts trout but also instantly signals takes. Then it's up to the angler; the quicker his reaction time, the more trout he will catch.

STRIKE INDICATORS

Some anglers don't like strike indicators. Many even find them aesthetically questionable. They are hard to cast, they do spook fish, and they often impede the natural drift of the fly, but very few fly fishers have ample focus and dexterity with the rod to not use them. I know only three: rod builder Bob Widgren, my brother Jackson, and my son Nick. They take up slack—just the slack, never pulling on the fly—by raising the rod as the fly drifts down toward them. They look for the line to tighten and set the hook when it does.

Focusing that hard is a lot of work, and those of us incapable of such concentration use bobbers. Strike indicators are our link with the underwater world and, as such, deserve attention here. First, no matter what type of indicator you use, it needs to be properly placed on the leader. One common mistake that many fly fishers make is putting their indicators next to the fly line. The thickness of the leader, plus kinks and slack spots, make transmission of information between bobber and fly slow and unreliable. Always place the indicator as close to the fly as possible and move the indicator up or down the leader at the same time that you change weight for different depths and currents.

Small paste-on indicators will fit through the rod guides and allow you to get flies snagged in the river (see page 24). The best indicators, however, are the cloth type that can be tied on with a slip knot. They are very sensitive and send clear messages as to what's happening in the depths. The round plastic bobber indicators are great if you have to do a lot of mending. Using a large dry fly as an indicator has a similar effect.

When nymphing upstream, always try to keep your indicator in the same current as your fly. When they are in different flows, there will be drag, or slack, between the two. Any slack between fly and indicator will prevent you from knowing when a fish takes because the creature will spit the fly out before the leader pulls tight against the indicator. This is actually a common occurrence, and countless trout are missed because of it. Of course, it is best to fish in such a way that this doesn't happen. Avoiding slack isn't always possible, so if you're having that problem, try putting two indicators on your leader. If you space them a couple of feet apart, they will help you keep track of what is going on and then keep excess slack from forming. Use different-colored paste-ons. For example, if a green one is upstream of a red, you know that things are flowing along in good order. If they are backward, something is awry.

This fish will take and eject the fly, but the angler won't know anything about it because of slack between indicator and fly.

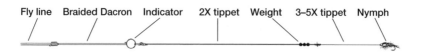

A deep-water nymph rig.

GET DOWN!

When nymphing in deep water, thin leader material will get a fly down quicker than a thick tapered leader. Consequently, less weight is needed, and less weight makes for more natural drifts. If you fish a lot of deep, fast water, try this rig: Tie a 2- or 3-foot butt section of braided Dacron fly-line backing to the fly line; below the Dacron use several feet of 2X tippet, then tie on your standard terminal tippet down to the fly; you can place weight above the tippet knot, and the indicator can go near the Dacron-2X connection; use a substantial indicator—a real cork one, perhaps—that will act as a buoy. The supple Dacron can be mended and moved this way and that without jostling the big, stable bobber. Long drifts, necessary in deep water, are then possible. This is, of course, an abominable setup to cast, so come way around in a circle when you sling it—and duck just in case.

If the fish are deep, be sure to cast far enough upstream of their suspected lie so that the fly has a chance to sink into position. Incidentally, this is usually farther than most anglers think. Be sure to use the right amount of weight. A really good nymph fisherman will change weight often, sometimes at each pool. How much weight? The rule of thumb is that the fly should touch bottom, or fish, occasionally. If you are hitting bottom all the time and getting snagged a lot, you are using too much weight. If your fly makes a few drifts without touching bottom, increase the weight.

Have a box of assorted small split shot and B shot—that's B, not BB—for deeper water. Clamp the shot above the tippet knot some 10–18 inches above the fly so that it doesn't slide down. If the shot slides down to the fly, trout will avoid it. Soft lead works well in places where you want the fly to sink slowly, like in gradually deepening riffles. Lots of good fishermen use twist-on lead, but it is not my preference. Personally I have all but eliminated the use of extra weight on my nymphs. Instead, I change to flies with different-size beads—or use ones with tungsten beads. (Sometimes I just add a piece of tippet to the tail fly and put on another fly for more depth.)

I used to think that the dry/dropper combo was best only for shallow water, but I have learned to run a heavy beadhead on several feet of tippet for deep water. Use a dry that is going to float the heavy nymph (like the Royal Stimulator). A lot of fish, even sophisticated ones, will eat these juicy flies, making this "hopper-dropper" rig the weapon of choice of guides almost everywhere. It seems to catch more fish than just a nymph with an indicator. This is partly due to the fact that the bobber (the dry) has a hook in it and catches fish, but the nymph produces more hookups, too, probably because of its close proximity to the dry—which telegraphs the strike instantly.

Admittedly my guides and I get so attached to fishing this setup that we could probably catch more fish than we suspect with just a dry—if we could tear ourselves away from the dry/dropper, that is. I suspect that the fish see the nymph first and so eat it; but many of them might come to the surface for the dry if they hadn't already been deceived by the nymph.

SUBTLE STRIKES

Although a telltale sign of a big fish taking a nymph is a very solid stop or sideways movement of the indicator, most strikes are subtle. So when that indicator bounces, stops, jiggles, shakes, twists, shimmies, dips, or dives, assume it's a fish and fire away at the least provocation. Often it's just the bottom, but if the fly is that deep, it is time to get it up and out of there anyway. Many of my clients don't react to a nudge on the indicator when their fly is drifting through shallow rocky spots because they think it is bottom, nor do they think a trout would be in such thin water. If that happens once and doesn't happen on subsequent casts on drifts through the same place, you can be sure it was a fish. I'm always generous about pointing this out to clients.

REMEMBER THAT THE INDICATOR DOESN'T HAVE A HOOK

The ever-so-intelligent trout sometimes shuns our cleverly tied flies and eats the strike indicator instead. They especially like orange. When this happens, your natural reaction is to set the hook. Because there is no hook in the indicator, ripping the thing out of its mouth will only spook the fish. If you can avoid striking, the fish may take the fly on the next cast.

HEAVILY FISHED WATER

Fishing nymphs in heavily fished water is the number one way to consistently catch tough trout. Even a group of fish huddled up in deep water and not really eating will have a member or two of the clan that will ingest a little beadhead that comes close by. The most productive setup for each river will usually be unique to that water. On the San Juan, guide John Tavner showed me that, at normal flows, a two-fly, 8-foot-long rig with a couple of No. 4 shot will catch fish in the deep and slow parts of most of the river. The flies are often an emerger of some dark and small design and a San Juan worm. Something big and bright with a bead draws the attention, and then a realistic tiny fly trails a foot behind.

A large cloth (or Thing a ma Bobber) indicator is usually used for such a rig in deep water. But don't be a slave to indicators because they can spook fish in shallow water. Use longer leaders and unobtrusive indicators—like a mono coil—for fish that may be frightened by a bobber landing on their heads. Just the other day we were nymph fishing and came upon a good fish that was out in the open sunlight. My client cast, and the large strike indicator spooked the big rainbow before it ever hit the water. Because this fish was clearly visible, we should have taken the indicator off. We could have seen the fish eat the fly anyway. (When you can see the body of a trout cruising, cast a single small nymph ahead of the fish so it sinks to its level, and then watch for its mouth to open and set the hook.)

Dry-Fly Fishing

When trout take a dry fly, they rise up to eat it and don't eject it until they return to their feeding station. The best time to set the hook is when the fish is heading downward. Consequently, a somewhat leisurely strike is best. If the dry is small—under No. 18—set the hook gently, especially if you are using a stiff rod, so the tiny gap doesn't rip through the fish's flesh.

The two-fly rig, made up of a good floating dry and a beadhead nymph dropper, is standard fare these days, but not many anglers are familiar with the joys of fishing two dries. It's a great setup when the trout are taking something small and hard to see because you can put it behind a more-visible fly. Tie the tail fly 3 feet behind the lead fly. The closer fly will absorb a lot of the drag, giving the tail fly a good float.

In Argentina, the willow-lined Malleo is one of the world's best dry-fly rivers.

When it is hard to see your smaller fly because of fast water or low light, use the hand fly as a locator. If anything "funny" happens near the hand fly, set the hook. Attaching a tiny piece of paste-on strike indicator 2 feet above a small dry can be helpful at times, too. Of course, another advantage of fishing two flies is that it isn't long before you start seeing that one is preferred over the other. In that case, you may want to fish two of the preferred flies.

DRY-FLY HOTSPOTS

All rivers have spots where fish are likely to be found rising when they are not coming up elsewhere. These are usually shallows, foam lines, places where currents sweep against bends, eddies, and natural funnels. There is no black-and-white description of these spots, but more food will be floating there than anywhere else. Quite often these spots are in a protected nook out of the prevailing winds, where insects are not swept away on the breeze. If you fish a section of river often, you get an intuitive feel for when fish will be rising in these places. If you love to fish dries, head to the river on calm and overcast days when insects are active and trout are not shy about rising.

SKATING IN THE WIND

Trout don't usually rise when it is windy because insects are unavailable if they are blown off the water, and the choppy surface makes the insects harder for the fish to see.

But at certain times it is smart and fun to skate dries on the wind. This is a marvelous way to fish caddis hatches, such as the Mother's Day hatch on the Rio Grande in New Mexico and on the Arkansas in Colorado. It is important to truly skate the fly in these situations, which means holding the rod high and fishing short, so that line and leader are in the air and only the fly is on the water. You can raise and lower the rod as wind gusts require; so that the fly bounces across the surface at an even pace, the fly should go as slowly as possible so the fish don't miss it. Use a 9-foot rod and flies with stiff hackles and hair, such as the Solomon Hair-Wing Caddis. Because trout often miss the fly, skate it slow enough for them to catch it. Also, don't always set the hook at the

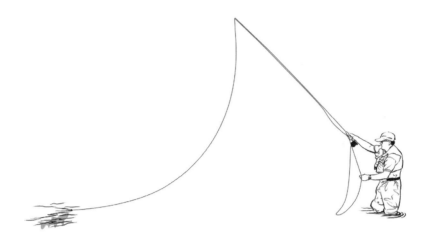

Skating dries is about as fun and exciting a way to fish as there is. It's best done with less than 20 feet of line.

sight of the rise. Instead, sometimes it's better to watch the curve of the line and leader; when it tightens, set the hook.

Skating dries is especially effective in late evening, when fish are feeding on top. You may know this frustrating scenario: It is near dark, nice trout are rising everywhere, and you can't see your fly. Now is the time to use a trick I learned when I was a kid from famed Adirondacks guide Fran Betters. Take out your little flashlight and cut your leader back to where it gets thick—1X or so—and tie on a large dry. Then skate the fly over those hungry fish. When you hear, see, or feel something, set the hook. When the light gets that low and the fish are eating like mad, the wisest old fish in the stream are easily fooled.

Fran and I used to pass over a certain bridge pool on the way to and from our own personal watering hole. We were usually in a hurry to get to our ultimate destination and consequently fished the bridge pool on the way home, when time meant little and it was dark and drunk out. We'd grab a rod out of the back of the car, cut the leader down to about 1 foot, and drag a huge dry across the surface of the pool below us. When we hooked one of those big bridge browns, we'd hand-line it up across the railing so as not to break the rod.

The numero uno food item for South American trout? Pancora.

Skating dries is a great way to fish in windy Patagonia also. At the suggestion of master guide Jorge Trucco, I tie a dry pancora crab imitation and skate it. Jorge told me that large trout often chase pancora, crayfish-like critters, to the surface, where they skip along in a panic. If you have seen some of those huge browns in the Argentine, you can understand the pancoras' terror.

FLAT-WATER

Many anglers are seduced by the tranquility of slow pools. Despite their allure, these places are not usually very productive except to the skilled caster. If pools have fast water at their heads, that is where the fish will do the bulk of their feeding because a greater volume of food lives and passes by there. You can figure out where the trout are going to be in such fast water because there is character in the form of rocks, different-speed currents, and edges. Fish in slow water can't be located as easily because their whereabouts are unknown in a featureless pool. Furthermore, because slow-water fish are constantly moving, if one does show itself, the rascal will probably be elsewhere by the time you get a cast to it.

Another concern in slow water is that trout have all the time in the world to inspect your fly to make sure they are getting the genuine article. Fast-water fish are easier to fool because they have to decide whether or not to eat quickly, before the meal washes away. Anglers also have an advantage in swift water because mistakes are masked by the water's turbulence.

These slow pools are a favored location when the fish are rising because you can easily spot trout and tell their size in flat water. This becomes particularly important when the light is bad, so when you expect a good evening hatch, make a plan that finds you in a long, slow pool at the end of the day. You'll be able to see both the fish and your fly much better than you will in fast water. When it gets so dark that you can't see much, don't stop fishing. That is when the big galoots turn reckless. The trick at that hour is to skate the fly and set the hook by sound and feel.

FLAT-WATER RISERS

Some people enjoy tough fishing for rising trout. I was raised on it. I used to fish with a famous dry-fly fisherman named Herb Dickerson on the Ten Mile River in New York State. (Herb took me fishing and hunting when I was a boy and collaborated with fly-fishing author Eric Leiser on some of his great fly books.) We would sit on the bank and wait for risers. It was a most proper way to fish in the English tradition of the sport. It was frustrating duty for an impatient boy some evenings—but it's also the best way to fish flat water in rivers because that is the only time fish show themselves.

Trout do much of their feeding on the surface in eastern streams, and many of our dry-fly traditions have come from there. It is an

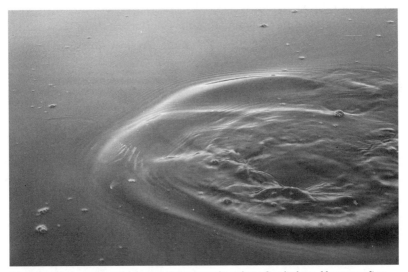

A big help is knowing which way the quarry is going after it rises. You can often tell by examining the rings of the rise. Rising fish push water ahead of them. Whichever way the wave is greatest is the direction the fish is heading. This fish is headed to the left.

addictive and challenging game. And anglers from that school can use their skills worldwide.

For instance, on the Chimehuin River near Junin de Los Andes in Argentina there is an accessible pool named Mananzo Pool. It is heavily fished—for the Argentine—but has risers every quiet summer evening. But they rise out a ways, and there are conflicting currents. It takes a small dry on a long and light leader to catch 'em. You can walk a half-mile downriver and find pretty dumb trout; but fly fishing is often a game much like golf, and many fishermen warm to difficult fishing. But you gotta be good and then lower your standards and consider a couple of fish to be a banner day.

I like it myself, so I have done a lot of it, and here are a few tips that I have gleaned.

When you find a group of steady risers, try to fish to them from the bank if you can. But closer is better for accurately casting and having a drag-free float—as well as for hooking and playing fish. So if you have to get in amongst 'em, wade into position *ever so slowly*. Try taking one foot out of the water at a time and with the toe entering the water first. Or shuffle your feet along at an even and very slow pace. The fish may stop rising anyway, but if you have gone carefully enough, they will go back to feeding in a few minutes. Wait until they are rising steadily again and target one good fish (you might as well fish for a big one because they are all going to spook when you hook one). Make the cast just to one side of, and slightly above, the fish.

Another option with a group of risers on slow water is to fish not for the largest, but for the closest one. Cast farther as you catch, or put down, each. This is a good idea if the fish are spread out, and you can pull one out without spooking the others. Always remember to halt activity when the fish stop rising. They will tolerate only so much, and the lower the light and the more intense the feeding, the more likely they are to return to eating promptly.

EMERGERS

In rivers that are fished hard it is common to catch one fish right off and then no more—even though the fish continue to feed. That's because in some waters they have to eat when people are around because there are always people around. They just go into a cautionary mode that is hard (but not impossible) to break. This is when you start changing flies. A fly just under the surface might catch one or two more. Have a tiny dry 1 foot in front of it for a strike indicator. If you can see the fish and need a very delicate presentation, use *just* the emerger. (Rub mud onto the fly and leader so the fly sinks—or soak it in your mouth for a moment.) Then as it is drifting down, watch the floating end of your leader—if you see it go down fast, set the hook gently. This works only if you are close.

OCCASIONAL RISERS AND ROAMERS

Trout that rise once in awhile in flat water are ones that are likely to be moving as well. This often occurs at the start of a hatch when there are only sparse insects. Such trout may turn more catchable when they get into a steady position as the bugs get more numerous. But lots of fish make their living on the roam and may eat whatever comes by—draw their attention with a small terrestrial, like a grasshopper or cricket.

For delicate fish on flat water, give them a beetle; and for yet more troublesome ones, go down to thinner tippet and use an ant. When prospecting for a roving fish, plop the fly on your side of its range and then make each cast just a little longer. Don't make more than a half-dozen casts because that will be counterproductive. (Because you usually don't know where such a trout is, you may line 'em and consequently spook 'em.)

When all this fails, get the fly in hand and simply wait. Have a few feet of line out and be ready, and when one rises, cast ASAP! Use one stroke—and drop it close to the rise. If you make a couple of false casts, the fish will be too far away! Or keep your line in the air and then bean it when it shows again. Unfortunately, such occasional feeders are sometimes disinterested trout that frighten easily. Give it up after a few minutes and go fish another spot. The instinctive fly fisher will quietly back out before the fish is thoroughly spooked; but allot time for it on the way back to the truck. Already knowing something of its habits, the crafty fly fisher will have a serious advantage over the reclusive trout if it has gone back to feeding.

Under some circumstances it is best to present the fly from upstream of a rising fish. That is the preferred method for difficult, leader-shy trout in flat water. But making the perfect cast that drops the fly just right is difficult. Instead, cast beyond where the fly needs to be, raise the rod, and pull the fly toward you. After you have got it straight upstream of the riser, lower the rod, thereby delivering the fly into the fish's jaws. Of course, have enough slack in the line so that the fly reaches the fish without drag. Add slack by shaking line out of the rod. Do this by holding the rod close to the water and waving it back and forth.

If fishing with a dry downstream, raise the rod slowly to set the hook, allowing the fish time to turn and close its mouth so that you aren't pulling the fly directly out of its open mouth.

When your fly has drifted past the riser, let it get a few feet farther and then tighten the line and let it swing directly downstream in the current. So as not to make a ruckus, retrieve it in some, raise the rod slowly, and lift the fly off the water gently. Note that when you are fishing downstream to risers, these ever-so-smart trout have a bothersome penchant for taking the dry fly as it swings out at the end of drift. Such surprises are often broken off by a spontaneous hook set on the tight line and thin leader.

Shake rod from side to side to feed line.

Watch a rising trout and see what it does when your fly goes over it. The more interest the fish shows and the closer it comes to your fly, the closer you are to having the right imitation. Avoid putting the same fly over the fish repeatedly because if the fish sees the fly and doesn't take it, it will be unlikely to consume it

This fish "felt" the plop of a hopper and swam 20 feet to get it.

on subsequent casts. A lot of activity only frightens the fish, so go ahead and change flies after just two or three good floats over the trout—or go find a dumber fish. If you stay with that trout, though, take your time. If it stops rising, don't cast until it starts rising again.

A great way to fish quiet water is to team up with another angler. One of you spots the fish, and the other tries to catch them. That strategy requires a high bank that overlooks the water. One guy spots cruising trout from above and instructs the other as to where to cast. This strategy can be productive, but the individual's fishing time is cut in half because politeness dictates that the spotter and the angler trade places. If you want to catch all the fish yourself, hire a guide and let him do all the spotting.

When you are sight fishing with grasshoppers in slow water, be careful not to smack the big fly right on the fish's head. The great thing about a hopper is that fish feel the fly plop and will travel a good ways to take it. So drop the fly a few feet to your side of the fish. Choose hoppers that will plop like a natural. I had a client who fished for a very long trout that was cruising under a grassy bank looking for hoppers in a shallow pool in Argentina. The fellow cast 20-plus feet short of the fish, and I was about to tell him to get it closer when, to our amazement, the trout turned toward the fly, casually swam straight at it, found it, and ate it. The best hopper fishing usually occurs in the late afternoon when it's warm and windy. Sun followed by scattered clouds would be ideal because trout are more prone to rise when there is some shade.

DON'T BE A DRAG

Another common mistake is casting too far upstream of rising trout. And by the time the fly reaches the fish, it's dragging. If you have the casting skills, drop the fly right on the fish's head; the fish may eat it without thinking. Sometimes that's the only way to fool very selective fish.

Most fly fishers don't realize how often their fly is dragging. This is often because they are 30 or 40 feet away from it and can't see the little bit of drag—but the fish can. Trout often grab for dragging dry flies but miss them. I'm not sure if they decide that the fly is acting unnaturally and miss it on purpose, or if they misjudge it because of the drag and consequently hit behind it.

CAPITALIZE ON THE HATCH

When you run into a nice hatch, take advantage. Many hatches last for only fifteen minutes, so make them pay while you can. When there are multiple hatches, fish take little breaks to digest and stretch between meals.

FAST-WATER ADVICE

The faster the water, the less ranging the trout will do to feed. Because fish don't see the fly well in churning water, you should cover such areas thoroughly. Another tip about fishing really fast water with dries is to drop your fly just below the white water. Fish aren't in the white stuff, and the fly will only get sunk and lost there.

KEEP DRIES DRY AND BUOYANT

Wash and grease your fly after each fish. Drying crystals should be used religiously when fishing for risers with small, hard-to-float flies like Comparaduns.

The Swing

When I started fishing in Argentina I did what most of us *jankees* (Argentine pronunciation) do when we travel to a foreign destination: I did it my way. I worked hard wading against those big rivers, fishing dry flies and nymphs upstream, as is customary here in the States. I caught fish in a lot of places, but on the big, wild rivers I saw that my Argentine friends were catching more fish than I—with less effort—by fishing downstream. They were swinging nymphs, Woolly Buggers, and other streamers on both floating and sink-tip lines.

I suspect that swinging flies works well where the trout eat stuff that swims—minnows, sculpins, crayfish, and the Argentine version of the latter, the pancora. Swinging is also a great way to fish when the water is high or the fish aren't feeding. That style of fishing seems to work best on gullible trout.

Swinging often produces a lot more action than fish because the fly interests trout that either don't eat or strike short behind the fly. But as a lot of water gets covered and a lot of fish get to see the fly, plenty of them will end up caught.

GETTING INTO THE SWING

What exactly is swinging? At first glance it seems like a simple matter: Merely cast across the current and hold on tight as the fly swings around with the current. Plenty of trout are hooked just that way, too. But, as with all tactics, some folks catch a lot more fish doing this than others. The most successful learn to hang the fly over the fish in evenly paced currents. They don't simply hold the fly in the current right below them because that fools only small fish. Bigger trout like to grab the fly just as it is quartering downstream. The fish follow the fly across the current, and after it starts to slow they nail it. If the angler can maximize

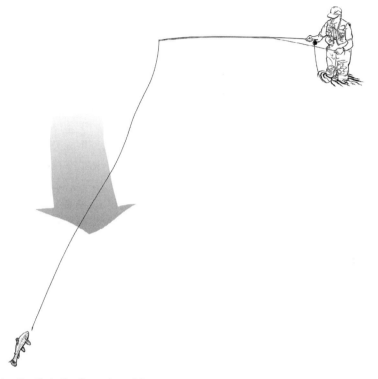

Hanging the fly in the "sweet spot."

that brief window when the fly hangs suspended during that quartering action, he will hook more fish.

Let's imagine a cast across a moderately fast and even current. When the fly starts swinging across the stream, the line forms a wide belly. That loop increases as the fly crosses the river, and by the time it is three-quarters of the way across the stream, it will zip along at such a rate that no fish will be able to catch it. That makes for a lot of short strikes. If, however, the fly swims back to your side of the river more slowly and hangs in the current, it will catch lots more fish.

The angler can accomplish this by wading out a little farther; ending the cast so that the rod is angled out in the river, thereby lessening the angle at which the fly swims; and mending and lifting line upstream so that it doesn't "bow."

DANCE THE ONE-STEP

This type of fishing is designed to cover a lot of water. At the completion of each cast the angler should wade downriver a step. British salmon fishermen have been doing this for centuries, proceeding at an easy, even pace. It sounds simple—cast, step, then cast, step again—but it takes more attention than one might imagine. My clients miss the beat of this little jig more often than not.

A common blunder is forgetting to step. They'll make three or four casts from the same spot and then, when they realize they missed the beat, take a couple of extra steps downstream to get back in rhythm. This concentrates the fly in one area and lessens their chances for action because the best odds are laid when new water is fished on every cast. Fish that are willing to take a fly that is swinging will be aggressive and probably don't need a lot of looks anyway. Certainly some pieces of water deserve more attention than others, but, in general, if you have lots of river to fish, try to cover new water with each cast.

Beginners and those folks who are slow to set a hook may do well on the swing because the fish pretty much hooks itself when it takes.

15

The Fly Fisherman or Fisherwoman

Most guides in the fly-fishing business will tell you that women are easier to teach than men. Women don't have as much tension in their arms—tension that is detrimental to fluid casting. Their egos aren't all bound up with being "top rod." I believe that these differences stem from the fact that women really don't care about "just fishing" and tend to enjoy nature more than men do. They'll even come right out and say, "I just like being here." This has been proven to me on many occasions when a woman would actually put aside her rod and sit down to enjoy the wild world around her—while the fish were biting! When I've suggested that it might be better to become inactive when the fish are in a like frame of mind, women have usually replied, "You go ahead and catch a few." That is not a common male response. Here is a little story to illustrate the male and female mentalities.

BLUEGILLS AND BOBBERS

During the drive to the stream, Bill tells one fishing story after another. These aren't bluegill-and-bobber stories. They're fish tales of high adventure—salmon beyond the Iron Curtain, billfish on the high seas, and huge sea-run trout of Tierra del Fuego. As we four-wheel over a jumble of rocks and roots he talks about night fishing for the man-eating catfish of the Amazon. Wife Gloria is in the back looking out the window, cool and disinterested, as if her husband's fishing stories have traveled this road before—in one ear and out the other. She volunteers that their friends fished at such and such a lodge and that their son worked as a guide one summer. She's certainly not unhappy with this trip into the New Mexico wilderness; she just seems, well, along for the ride.

Our hike to the water takes us through a virgin forest, which seems to inspire wonder in Gloria. She interrupts an epic tale about a marlin battle to ask the name of a tall, flashy wildflower. I tell her it's fireweed. Encouraged, I take Bill and Gloria a few feet out of the way to where a beaver is making slow but steady progress on a foul-tasting pine. The 3-foot-thick tree is gnawed about halfway through its trunk, and a crack that runs up the tree has formed. On the sway of each breeze the crack opens and closes as the giant moans its death song.

When we arrive at the stream, things look good. Mayflies are dancing up and down in shafts of light, and a couple of yellow Wilson's warblers flit about catching them. Bill glances at the surroundings and utters the gruesome phrase that strikes fear into the heart of every guide: "Just point me in the right direction. I can take care of myself." I give him a couple of flies and the tiny amount of instruction that I think he will accept and take Gloria for her first fly-fishing lesson. When away from Bill she confesses that she is doing this for him, as if I couldn't already tell, and that she will try it but asks me to go easy on her. I tell her that teaching is hard work and that the less of it I have to do, the better.

As opposed to a lot of men, most women anglers take the time to take in their surroundings and enjoy themselves—and delight in their catch!

She seems fairly bored with the fifteen-minute crash course in casting. Her attitude changes quickly, however, after she starts fishing because she somehow manages to drop her first cast onto a fish's head. With the 10-inch rainbow attached to her fly she emits screams, squeals, and giggles that echo off the canyon walls. She reels the trout right up to the end of the rod and is frantically grabbing for it. Of course, the 6-foot space between her hyperextended hand and the end of the 9-foot fly rod creates a comical problem. When I stop laughing I suggest that if she can't reach the thing, she'd better let out some line so that we can get at it. That is just the start of things. The little fishes are in such a reckless mood that she starts catching so many that it isn't long before I leave her on her own and go looking for the boss.

Bill is planted right where I had left him—and looking mighty out of place, zinging yards of line up the little brook. Any fish that might be interested in his fly—unlikely because it is dragging across several currents—would be thrown into a state of shock at the sight of his tall, well-postured figure towering over their home.

Before I have an opportunity to speak to him, his wife comes into view from downstream. She is now running on predatory instincts. We watch spellbound as she zeroes in on her next victim. She creeps low to the edge of the stream, slithers behind a boulder, and waves her magic wand over the water. True, her cast is pitiful—limp-wristed and floppy—but it is perfect in the fast-falling stream because her fly settles on the water with plenty of slack, giving the fly a drag-free float. A wild slash of the rod and a loud shriek mean she has hooked another. Hubby's ears turn red as he slams a double-haul to the next bend. This presents the perfect opportunity for me to do my job, and I try to suggest a more appropriate way for him to fish that little creek. He isn't too keen on making the "bad cast," and crawling is definitely beneath him, but before long he is slipping along the stream like a ten-year-old boy—and catching fish.

As we are preparing to leave, he hooks what looks like the fish of the day, but it comes loose at the water's edge. He pounces down onto the squiggling creature and pins it between his hands and knees. It pops out and into the drink. Because this is catch-and-release fishing

I am surprised to see Bill plunge in after the fleeing fish. After more squiggling, squirming, splashing, and crashing he raises the fish aloft for our admiration. The capture of that 14-incher seems to put the family hierarchy back in order, and he signals that it is time to go.

On the ride back Bill digs out a few more exotic fishing and hunting stories from far-off lands and waters. Gloria returns to her backseat position and adds, "That was fun. Let's do it again."

16

Reading Water

One reason why anglers do better with a guide than they do on their own is because a guide has them fish only high-percentage spots. The average unguided angler pounds all the water. The guide, however, has learned from experience which places actually produce. Sure, other spots may hold trout, but that doesn't mean they are going to yield them. The currents may be too confusing, the depths too great, or perhaps the setup is such that the fish always see you coming. One thing all honey holes have in common is they fish well. By that I mean these spots are situated so that a perfect approach and drift can be achieved.

FIND PRODUCTIVE SPOTS
How can you—Joe Q Fly Fisherman—find these places? It isn't easy; in fact, it is, without question, the hardest aspect of fly fishing to learn. Hiring a guide helps teach you to identify good water because you will usually be standing in it. Later, when you are on your own, you can look for similar spots. When it all starts coming together, the light will click on, and you will realize that certain sections of a river are much fishier than others. Obviously the best place to learn about water is on the river itself, but because you are currently reduced to reading these words, here are some observations that may be of use.

DEEP AND FAST WATER
An important fact to remember about deep and fast water is that the current is often much slower at the bottom than at the surface and that water that may appear to be too fast could actually hold some nice fish. Usually only large trout have the strength to inhabit heavy water. The problem is getting a fly down to them through the turbulence. Upstream nymphing is the method of choice because that style of fishing gets the

Although the water is raging at the surface, it may be much slower near the bottom and harbor big trout.

fly down the deepest. The fly will likely take a different course each time in such wild water, and it may take many drifts before it actually passes in front of the fish, so make plenty of casts if the spot looks really fishy. Also, fish the heavy, deep water from a couple of different positions because the fly will do different things from each. Use a tippet long enough for the fly to get down, and if you aren't getting strikes, or touching bottom occasionally, add lead.

UNDERCUT BANKS

Look for big browns where the current has undercut earthen banks, rocks, and tree roots. Those slimy devils like working undercover. Such spots are especially favored in late summer when rivers are low and hiding places scarce. The lusher the bank's grass, the happier the fish will be because there will be more shade and terrestrial insects. These spots are good choices during bright sunlight when the trout feel more comfortable tucked away under something.

Most anglers don't realize how close their fly needs to be to the bank, and I'm forever saying, "Closer. Get it in closer." The fish are under there for a reason, and they don't like to venture out very far to eat. The fly needs to float within inches of the bank.

The water is usually a bit slower right along the bank than out a foot or so, and getting a good float is not easy. If you are standing out in the main flow and casting in against the bank, the current you're standing in will drag your fly out of the slower current by the shore. Consequently, fishing the bank from the bank itself is usually best, and, as usual, the shorter the line you fish, the better the float. So get as close as possible, being sure to stand back from the edge a few feet so the fish don't see you, and walk softly so they don't hear you. This is especially important if the banks are soft and the current is slow.

Although the hopper-dropper rig is not easy to cast accurately toward the bank, it is otherwise perfect for this situation. The trout may be drawn to the hopper, but if it is dragging, it will be refused. Trout will, however, tolerate more drag on a submerged fly than a dry, and they often grab the nymph after they refuse the hopper. On occasions when the fish take the dry over the nymph, remove the nymph for greater casting accuracy.

SLOW-WATER STRATEGIES

Avoid featureless slow water unless fish are showing themselves by rising or cruising in the shallows; or you are on a tail water stream simply loaded with trout. Otherwise it is unlikely that a fly sent randomly into slow water will have the good fortune to encounter a trout. (See page 121 for suggestions on fishing flat water.)

PICK THE POCKETS

Boulder-strewn sections of river are great for the fly fisher who is willing and able to battle through them. Pocket water doesn't fish well from a distance, so aggressive wading is called for. Maneuvering streamers or

An angler wading close and reaching high with rod. *Nick Streit*

wet flies through the pockets works sometimes, but you will usually do better by fishing flies on a dead drift. To get that effective natural drift, however, you have to be close—close enough that the rod tip is over or near the pocket you are fishing.

This type of water tends to be of medium depth, so the hopper-dropper rig is usually the best choice. I like a big dry on top, even in late summer after the hatch, with a beadhead nymph underneath it. If the pockets are short and deep, don't be shy about running 3 or 4 feet of tippet down to the nymph. Be sure the nymph has a heavy enough bead—this is where tungsten beads are great—to reach the fish.

MATCH METHODS AND FLIES TO THE WATER

Choose methods and flies that match the water in which you are fishing. Look at and think about the water you are planning to fish. If it is generally shallow, you might want to think risers and fish it with dry flies. The hopper-dropper shines in knee-deep water. If the water is deep, use a heavy nymph. Woolly Buggers are great in tricky currents because they

Great water! The angler stands in medium-speed, calf-deep water with a current good for swinging the fly.

The white water is too fast to hold fish.

The fishing would be better just below the dropoff.

Look carefully for risers in the foam.

A funnel has a good chance of holding fish.

can be dead-drifted, sunk deep and jiggled, or maneuvered around rocks. Far too often I see anglers fishing in spots where they have little chance of success with the rig they are using. An example is fishing a shallow-running nymph in deep water. Some of my most successful days guiding are those when I carry a second rod that is rigged differently than the client's. That way we can fish two types of water effectively.

WHAT'S IT WORTH?

When you start to get a fairly good idea of where the fish are, the next step is knowing how many casts each spot is worth. This depends not only on how many fish the place holds but also on how many casts it requires to fish it effectively. The really skilled angler may walk a half-mile without ever making a cast and then throw a hundred times in one place.

INSTINCTIVE FLY FISHING

The final step of angling enlightenment comes when you find yourself hooking trout by gliding from pool to pool, without consciously following a selection process. When you have reached this stage, you've advanced—or is it reverted—to being an instinctive fly fisher.

17

Riffles

Riffles are fast, shallow water that runs over gravel and small rock. Because mayflies, caddis, and stonefly nymphs thrive in such locations, riffles are also where feeding fish congregate. Riffles that are connected to a pronounced pool are best because the deeper water of the pool provides protection from winter freeze-up, low water, and predators. Living is easy in such idyllic surroundings. The trout chill in the pool and then simply swim upriver when they get wind of a mayfly hatch. Riffles become even more important in rivers that suffer from heavy silt buildup because whereas the silt piles up in slower water, it is swept through the fast water of the riffle. Most insects do poorly in silt, and life is more concentrated in the riffles.

MAKE A PLAN

Unlike other sections of a stream where structure may direct you to fish, many riffles have uniform, unbroken flows and consequently offer few telltale signs. Consequently, fish them systematically to cover this precious water. Most anglers just step in and fire away. Sure, they may catch a fish or two, but if they had planned a strategy, they might have hooked many more. Stand on the bank for a moment and devise your plan. Most riffles are shallow at the head and deepen and slow as they descend. If you are fishing upstream with dries or nymphs, start just above the flat water, where the river starts to get shallow and has some movement. Work the riffle from right to left and, to avoid lining fish, make each cast a bit longer than the last. Never start with a long cast and then make subsequently shorter casts. Assume that fish will travel 1–2 feet to grab the fly and space your casts accordingly. But use a dense blanket of casts as you move up into the fastest water. The trout can't see well in the turbulence unless it is very close to them, nor will they move far to get the fly in fast water. Another reason to fish the heads of the riffles thoroughly is that the largest fish are often found there.

If the riffle is very expansive, fish it by wading back and forth across it a couple of times. I emphasize "wading" because if you physically move into position and cast straight upstream, you will get the best drift. (Actually, the cast should be just a few feet to your right if you're a righty.) If you make long casts across the current and then mend, the drift will not be as true as the upstream drift.

MAGIC CURRENT

Often you can find trout just about anywhere in a riffle, but a magic speed of current really attracts them. That favored water is usually below the really fast stuff, where the current begins to deepen and slow. A surface chop that is a couple of inches high and dances this way and that often characterizes such water. Plenty of food will be carried to the fish there, and they don't have to struggle against strong rapids to meet it. Also look for dropoffs near the head of the riffle because fish will sit in the slack water underneath the structure and grab food as it washes by them.

Angler with a good-size brown. This magic current speed is ideal for big fish.

If a lot of food is washing down, the fish may get ravenous and move into very fast water to feed—or at least they may appear to be in very fast water. Actually, trout use tiny breaks in the current to escape the powerful head-on flow. When looking for these spots remember that even a big trout is only a few inches wide and that the faintest break can hold a fish. In most rivers, though, it is rare to find fish in the really fast stuff (except in rich tailwaters). The lazy critters are much more likely to be found on the edges of the riffles—looking for that medium-speed current they love. When you study a riffle be conscious of this fact because many are simply so fast that the fish are reduced to living on the edges.

If there isn't much edge, there won't be many fish.

Even if you are familiar with a riffle, check it out each time you fish it because changes in flow levels will dictate your quarry's position in the riffle. High flows push fish to the sides, and lower flows move them into the middle and up into the faster water.

18

Eddy Fishing

Big trout do very well in eddies. It's an easy life: no fast water to battle; food conveniently circulating; and a blanket of foam providing overhead security. More importantly, trout are seldom removed from eddies because few fly fishermen know how to fish these great spots. Most anglers mindlessly throw straight casts into eddies from too far away, and the fly and line drag across the revolving currents and alarm the fish.

THE SECRET OF BEING CLOSE

Eddies come in various shapes and sizes, so each requires an individual strategy, but most call for your getting close enough that your rod tip is actually over the eddy. (The exceptions here are big eddies in large rivers.) Because the current along the bank is really running upstream, casting downriver to get a proper drift is necessary. Be careful, however,

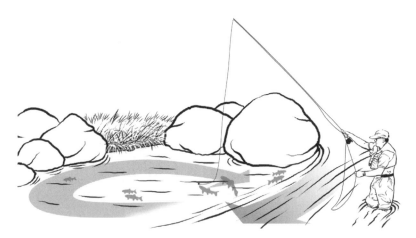

When fishing a dry in an eddy, put just your fly onto the water—no line, no leader. Fish don't usually spook across a fast current, and this angler has a low profile from this position.

144

because fishing from the bank puts you up high where the fish may see you. Either kneel or hide behind something.

It is often possible to wade close to the eddy from midriver and then reach across the fast water to drop your fly from there. This is a good approach because it gives you a low profile. You can get much closer than you might suspect because trout seldom spook when fast water separates you from them.

Silt buildup is common in eddies, so if you must stand in the revolving current be careful not to stir a warning of liquid dust ahead of you.

FISHING THE FOAM

When approaching an eddy that has a layer of foam on it, study the foam carefully because trout can often be found rising in the suds—even on days when fish are not coming up elsewhere. These fish, although often big, can be hard to spot because the food they are munching is usually dead, and only slight effort is needed for them to take spent insects in slow water. The rise of even a large fish may manifest itself as only a little nudge of the suds.

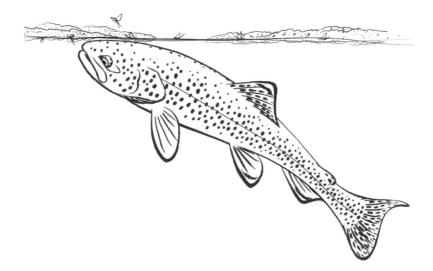

When you come to a foam eddy, watch it carefully before casting. Chances are good a trout will be in there, feeding undetected.

A few problems are inherent in presenting a dry fly in thick foam. One is that the foam and debris may muck up the fly. Another is that the fly may ride on top of the foam instead of flush at the surface, like the naturals do. In addition, the fish may have a hard time seeing your imitation in all that foam, in which case it is wise to get the fish's attention by slowly skating the fly over it. For the fly to look natural, there should be no line or leader on the surface. You must be very close to do this, but fish won't see you if the foam is thick. If the dry doesn't work, drag a lightly weighted nymph in front of the rising fish. As in any situation when fishing for rising trout, if they stop coming up, stop fishing for them. If you rest the spot, the fish will usually begin rising again in a few minutes.

GET TO THE BOTTOM OF THINGS

Eddies are often very deep, and the fish will not always be near the surface. The best way to get a fly down to them while maintaining the all-important dead drift is from the same close position you use with a dry fly. My brother Jackson Streit showed me this tactic: Take a heavy, beadhead Woolly Bugger and send it straight down into the depths. Do this by lowering the rod at the same rate that the fly is sinking. If you lower the rod too fast, slack will be created in your leader, and you won't feel a fish grab the fly. I have shown this technique to a thousand guided clients, and 90 percent of them will just flop the fly and leader down in a pile. At this point I want to scream because I know a huge trout is inhaling the fly—on a slack leader—and there is no way for us to know anything about it topside. Practice lowering the fly into water where you can see it descend, and you will learn the proper pace. This is also a great way to fish other deep spots, such as undercut banks and deep swirling pockets.

After the Woolly Bugger reaches bottom, jig it with the rod tip as it circulates the eddy. The fly will do its best work when it is straight down from the rod tip, and you may be able to walk it around the eddy if you think you won't spook the fish. When finished with the drift, don't just yank the fly from the bottom to the top with a quick move. Give any fish that might be eyeing it a chance to eat by jiggling the

Jigging an eddy can sometimes result in big fish.

tantalizing morsel all the way back to the surface at a slow, even pace. Try this maneuver for any predatory fish because lust often overtakes such impulsive creatures, and they grab the meal just as it is about to leave their domain. You can fish nymphs and streamers in these places, too, but Woolly Buggers are wonderful teasers, with that sexy marabou swaying back and forth.

19

Ponds and Lakes

Most guided clients prefer fishing moving water, and that's under-standable because it is generally more interesting than fishing ponds or lakes. Still waters, however, offer a nice contrast to the chaos of mov-ing water. And ponds are often at their best when rivers are unfishable, such as during spring runoff. Also, because the little fishies that live in still water don't have currents to battle, they grow more quickly into big fishies.

FISHING PRESSURE

Fishing pressure is a critical issue on ponds and lakes because the fish can nose up to a fly and inspect it as if it were under a microscope. If they've been hooked in the recent past, the trout will be very difficult to fool. I have a couple of ponds that I use for guiding, and we try not to put too much pressure on them so the denizens don't get suspicious. If you don't have that option, and you find yourself fishing for difficult trout, use smaller flies, thinner tippets, and slow—or no—retrieves.

READ THE WATER

You can't read still water like you can a stream. Getting a good overview of a lake is helpful, and if a nearby hill provides a promontory, ascend it and look down for dropoffs, shallows, and other structures that will concentrate food and fish. If the lake is shallow, it will probably fish well with floating lines. Conversely, if it is deep, plan to get down to them with sinking lines. Look for inlets and outlets because they can prove to be key fishing spots. For example, if there is a good hatch in the feeder creek, fish will gang up at its mouth.

If the wind and light are conducive to good visibility, sight fishing is an exciting and productive way to fish. Look for elevated shorelines

Inlets and outlets are always worth checking because they're often productive.

from which to fish because it is easier to spot cruising trout from above. If the fish is close to the surface, it may take a dry fly. If it's several feet deep, tie on a beadhead nymph and cast it far enough in front of the fish that it intercepts the fish and sinks to its level. The fly needs to be on a collision course with the trout because it usually won't come upward very far to take it. Don't move or watch the fly; look at the fish. If it is coming for the fly, it will speed up a little and change course. When you see the whites of its jaw open, set the hook. Use a single nymph in this situation and tie it to a long leader and tippet, so if the fish is deep, the fly will be free to sink quickly.

Of course, you can't very well sight fish if you can't see fish. Some folks are better than others at spotting them. Always walk slowly and study the water carefully. Usually feeding fish will be on the move, and that is the giveaway. If you think you see something that looks fishy, but you're not sure, cast to it quickly. Many times I see clients pondering whether they are seeing something—as the "something" swims away. After years of fishing I have learned to trust my initial instincts in these matters: If I think that I saw something, I probably did.

The fish love to cruise along shorelines and next to and over weed beds, so it may be a good idea to cast along this structure and retrieve a fly parallel to it. Although structure is not as important to trout as it is to bass, for example, they love the shade and will be found under trees. They are not there to ambush prey like a bass would be but more to have the overhead protection and the food falling from the trees.

Using a dry/dropper combination is a great way to fish rivers, but that setup works well in still waters, too. The trick is to have the nymph at the appropriate depth. That may range from a few inches to a few feet. In the rather common case of trout rising for emerging midges, I like to put the little subsurface emerger only a foot behind a small dry. For example, a No. 16 Elk Hair Caddis with a light tan wing is very visible, and midging fish will often take it.

FISHING IN A TUBE

Fly fishing from a tube is easy living, maybe even downright lazy. Unfortunately, most folks don't get into the spirit of it and work their

Trolling from a tube can be a deadly tactic.

butts off by casting repeatedly. Whether fishing dry or wet flies, you'll find it more productive to keep your fly in the water than in the air.

I have found it best to have my clients troll wet flies from the tube rather than cast them about randomly. (Unless they are casting at fish or some sort of quality structure.) Trolling is effective because the fly is always in the water, and your hands and rod are always in position to set the hook. And if you are fishing deep, your fly will be at that effective depth all the time. The alternative, constantly casting and retrieving, puts the fly into the air, sinking toward the proper depth, or rising away from it, keeping it where it belongs only half the time.

When fishing dry flies, cast to the area that the fish are working and don't move the fly. Sure, it gets boring to stare at a dry for minutes on end, but remember that the fish are on the hunt for something to eat and that they will eventually find your offering. When they do, it will be in a still, natural state. I find that the clients who are patient about this will outfish those who cast here and there.

In Argentina we do a lot of fishing from a motor boat, and, with the fishing pressure being so light there, the trout seem unafraid of the motor's noise. We cruise just off the shorelines under power and retrieve large grasshopper flies that are cast toward shore. This is much like bass fishing with a popping bug. From that fishing I learned how important it can be to get a trout's attention by popping or twitching a fly. When a fish is swimming by your dry fly but shows no notice of it, give the fly a little twitch. But be careful not to make it too vigorous a twitch and sink it.

Unless they are rising to something distinct and easy to replicate like a Callibaetis mayfly, use a cast of two wet flies rather than a dry because you don't know precisely where the fish are, and two retrieved flies cover the most water. And trout that might closely inspect a dry will often pounce on a wet. Slap the cast a couple of feet to the side of the rise and retrieve the fly just a yard or two, and then quickly, using the "lift-and-snap," drop it on the other side of the rise. Repeat the process one more time but a few feet farther from the fish's last known whereabouts. After that, it's anybody's guess as to where it is.

Good lake flies for this seem to be lightly weighted damsel nymphs, dragonfly nymphs, or dark Woolly Buggers for the first fly. Use a much smaller nymph 3 feet back for the tail fly. Use something with a small bead in a dark shade—zug bug, peacock nymph, or pheasant tail.

When wading out from the bank in a lake most anglers fish only out to the deeper water. But remember to look for fish in the shallow water because this is often where the largest and hungriest fish feed.

SCOUT FOR TROUT

Trout in lakes often patrol in circular patterns. If you can get yourself in a position to physically see fish cruising, you will get an idea of how fast and where they travel. Because their speed and patterns are fairly universal, your observations will help you outwit them in similar situations elsewhere.

In the last couple of years I have been wearing binoculars when fishing. They come in handy for many tasks, but their greatest use is for spotting rising fish. I had often walked great distances to where I'd seen trout rising, only to discover when I got there that they were dinks. With the optics you can usually tell from afar if the fish are worth going after.

Big fish leave bulky riseforms and tend to show body parts when they come up. They push the water in waves in front of them; the heavier the wave, the heavier the fish. Another good use of the binoculars is to see other anglers. See where they are fishing, and head the other way. But then, you already knew to do that.

20

Hiring a Guide

Connecting fisher and fish by a mere thread is an age-old miracle. But as anyone who has ever wet a line can attest, it is not so easily done. So people pay a guide to make it happen. But what exactly does a guide trip entail?

First, a guide has to choose the place that suits the fisher—his or her skill and level of physical fitness. So the guide needs to know miles of water and how it fishes under different conditions for different people. Then, the guide must know which aquatic insects are hatching and which of the thousand flies in his pocket will fool the trout. When finally standing in said water, the real work begins, and with the client's blessing, the guide gets hold of the client's elbow and gently "guides" him or her into the exact position to fish the spot. It is a rare occurrence when the fly lands in the jaws of awaiting fish, and so a little casting coaching may be necessary at this point. After the fly is deposited onto the water it then needs to drift on the bouncing and twisting currents. If it "drags," maneuvers like mending, reaching, and high sticking are taught. And when the fish opens its mouth to eat the fluffy fake, the client often lets out a whoop. Although professionally reserved at this commonplace event, a good guide inwardly whoops, too, because we *never* tire of attaching fisher to fish—it's always a wonder—and just by a thread.

And hiring a guide is a great way to get around the nonsense of our apparently complicated sport and cut straight to the chase. You'll probably catch plenty of fish, but, more importantly, you'll learn a lot. Of course, a guide can start beginners on the right foot, but people with moderate experience will benefit even more. Most have a head full of questions to be answered. Another angler who can be helped a lot is the city-bound fellow who endlessly reads scientific and technical books on fly fishing. Such an expert is often in serious need of "de-education," and the experienced guide will help him sort through the jumble of info to point out what really matters. Such an overqualified angler will walk away from the river freed of the burden of insignificant details.

FIND THE RIGHT GUIDE

However, you need a wise guide for this task. How do you find such a reclusive varmint? You can check chambers of commerce, state game and fish offices, the Web, fly shops, telephone directories, and so on. This will get you a list from which to choose, but remember that great fishermen are like artists: The best are seldom good businessmen and self-promoters and thus may be hard to find—or may have all the business they can handle. Call your fishing friends or acquaintances near where you are going. It won't matter whether they fish or not; they have probably heard the name of the best guide in town.

After you have identified your wily guide, consider your options before contacting him. First, don't shoot yourself in the foot by limiting your choices—"I want to fish a meadow stream for big fish, with dry flies, of course. I picture a tall tree on the left bank with some high peaks in the background . . ." Your poor guide will have racked his little brain all night thinking of an appropriate place to take you, and he—or she—won't be of much use come daylight. It is okay to suggest the type of fishing you would like, as broadly as possible, but try not to get too specific. It is certainly a legit question to ask about the size of fish—but if big fish are important to you, ask well before your trip so private water could be arranged. (See Chapter 27, "Maps.") If you want a relaxed guide working for you, say that you want to learn as much as possible, catch a few fish, and have a pleasant day. This information will ground your neurotic guide and give him sufficient choices to ensure a successful day's outing. You might also ask your guide if he has the proper permits for the area (state, National Forest, and BLM) and if he is insured. Because if all the permits aren't in place your fishing options may be limited. Such inquiries will also weed out inferior renegade guides.

The author being inducted into the Freshwater Fishing Hall of Fame. He is flanked by author John Nichols (left) and Elmer Guerri (right).

MAXIMIZE THE EXPERIENCE

When you get to the water, remember that most angling guides are control freaks who get frustrated by witnessing bad fishing and casting. We never know how folks are going to respond to suggestions, so by all means solicit help. I always breathe a sigh of relief when my client says, "Feel free to tell me when I'm doing something wrong."

Be careful not to paint yourself into a corner with your guide. Many times on the phone or in the car a guy goes on about all the places he has fished and all the great fish he has conquered. At water's edge, however, it may be found that mighty Captain Ahab can't cast past his shoe, making for a most awkward situation. Just how are you going to tell a big-game fisherman that he has to practice his 10-to-2 casting? We see few really good fly fishers, so don't worry about sounding inexperienced. After you are on the water, you can't fake it anyway.

What's really important for the guide to know before the trip is your conditioning and abilities. Knowing this will allow him to match you with the water that suits you best. Figuring out your age, health, and skill over the phone is tricky business, so volunteer as much relevant information about yourself as possible. Then the guide can match geographical handicaps to you. What might be a long hike or challenging fishing to some is a stroll to others. For instance, the best fishing we have in our neck of the woods is in the Rio Grande Box. But the river sits at the bottom of a 700-foot box canyon, and when the angler gets to this remote water there are then innumerable boulders to crawl over and around. And the fishing itself is technical. After a big rainbow is hooked, the fish often comes off unless the person has experience fighting fish in class 5 rapids. Everyone wants to go, but only a tiny percentage of our clients have the health, discipline, and fishing abilities to do it.

Westerners are used to covering a lot more ground on foot than are Easterners. And what constitutes fly-fishing expertise changes from east to west, too. Easterners can do surprisingly well in the West because they usually have a lot of time on the water. Many have streams out their back doors and compete with their neighbors every evening to catch sophisticated trout. Eastern fishermen's greatest shortcoming is that when they get into the wide-open spaces of the West they don't move enough.

Unfortunately, those who might benefit the most from a local guide don't hire one. These are folks who have been fishing an area for some time, taking what they consider to be good catches. There is a big difference, however, between fishing for fun and fishing professionally, and the local sportsman might have quite an eye-opening experience by fishing with an accomplished guide.

I feel I have had enough difficult jobs in my life to qualify as an expert on that four-letter word *work*. I've roughnecked in the oilfields, fought forest fires, made adobes, built houses, surveyed, retailed, and spent long, snowbound winters tying thousands of flies. Guiding, when done well, is physically, mentally, and emotionally the most draining of the lot. The job consists of long hours of being a naturalist, therapist, sage, valet, cook, historian, and babysitter. Yet, because the guide is perceived to be a guy "who gets paid to go fishing," the world offers little sympathy. Of course, the perks include making people laugh under the open sky and never tiring of seeing fish inhale a fly. The absolutely best guides don't care who is holding the rod when it happens. That's the guide for whom you're looking.

And please tip your guide well and remember that he could have a real job—perhaps he is employable—where he could work all year instead of just a few months. Many clients compute the fees they pay for guiding and think that we are racking it in and don't realize that, besides the short season, we are a business like any other and that there is plenty of overhead in the form of permits, insurance, advertising, freebie trips as donations, and so on. I have gone about as far up the guiding ladder as possible and will have to work until my dying day, it looks like.

As a tip guideline, on a $395 trip we usually get $50 to $60, but C-notes are very common. If you are a large group and have several guides, pool the money and then hand it to the guide in charge and ask him to distribute it.

FISHING SOLO

As an experienced fisherman, I can usually catch more fish if I'm fishing alone than with other people. This also holds true when fishing with a guide. One fisher and his or her guide can be flexible and go when conditions are right. When more people are involved, constraints of time, physical conditioning, and personality arise. Generally, the more people we have on a guide trip, the fewer the choices we will have as to where to fish. A large group will contain someone who can't walk, someone who can't fish, someone who wants to quit early, someone who wants to go to the gin mill, and someone who just came from the gin mill. If the fishing is more important to you than socializing, be thoughtful when choosing your fishing partners. Also consider that when you have a beginner on a guided trip, that person will need more of the guide's attention. Having a beginner along will also dictate the choices as to where to fish. Beginners should be put into water they can handle. This is usually fast water that requires short casts.

Advice for Guides

I conduct a guides school each spring, and it includes the elements that everyone expects: tying knots, casting, and finding fish. But part of my job is to teach students that, although it made the top ten dream jobs in *Outside* magazine, guiding is hard work. This news typically comes as a shocker. No one is going to pay them to fish, and watching others do it poorly can be downright painful! Which leads us to the fact that the guide's job is really much more about people than fish. So to have a good outing the guide has to shake these brutalities off and work on the client's skills.

START ON THE RIGHT FOOT

Be on time. In fact, show up a few minutes early so that you can find out from the lodge or fly shop about the trip, including what water is available. Be prepared before greeting the clients. Then inventory their gear, outfit them, and get them out the door.

Have everything you need so that you needn't make any stops after you're on the road.

Have a relatively clean vehicle and clean windows.

Be sure to give whatever tidbits of info that you have about the local and natural world. I used to hire a guy in Argentina—Lorenzo Sympson—who had never caught a fish in his life, but he was the facilitator of a condor study, and his overall knowledge of the natural world of Patagonia was so astounding that all clients were charmed.

When deciding where to go, ask the clients what they are looking for, that is, instruction, big fish, scenic places, few people, and so on.

If a hike is required, be sure to carefully explain it. I can't remember the number of clients who have said, "Just take me anywhere. I don't mind the walk" and then complained afterward about what a grueling trip it was. I have learned not to make a decision about where to fish until I lay eyes on the client.

If it's one of those trips where the wife doesn't want to fish very much, believe her: She probably doesn't! Let her sit on the bank and be happy. She'll fish when she feels like it.

We encounter many people who are convinced that paying profusely will bypass a need to know how to fish. Private water, if it's available, is usually the best solution for such clients.

When choosing a river or section of river, ask fishers if they are right- or left-handed because different sections of river fish better for one or the other.

Keep in mind that your clients—not you—have the rod in their hands and that although you could catch a sack full of fish in one place, they might be blanked and very frustrated by the experience.

I know a good fly fisherman who had a brief career in guiding. He left the trade disillusioned. A conflict arose because he, being fond of stalking large rising trout in still water, was very particular about the type of fishing he would *allow* his clients to do. He projected that challenge onto his clients only to find out that virtually none of them had the chops to do it, making everyone frustrated and fishless. He quit the job in disgust.

That's fine; the guiding profession doesn't need any more elitists. Real guiding is about taking care of the individual people and not about providing a voyeuristic exercise for the guide's benefit.

This past season I guided a fellow with a terminal illness: He was a first-time fly fisher, and he had to be held up so he didn't get washed downstream. He caught a 7-inch trout and said that he now was happy to die! Heavy business sometimes, this guiding.

Try to fish beginners and weak casters in fast water where you can get right up on the fish. It may be best to avoid going after big fish with beginners because they will only lose them and then be even more frustrated.

When you have two or three clients, fish them together and leapfrog from pool to pool. Canyon-type creeks may not lend themselves to such a plan, however, because there is usually not enough room to go around each other without spooking the trout. In most situations, though, when you have folks close together, you can stay in control and move them as necessary.

Never let one jackrabbit of a client get ahead and out of sight. You will have lost control and have no idea what water he has trashed for the other clients. Think of the clients as cows that need to always be in green pastures. Don't let any wander off, but when herding them, be careful.

HERDING HINTS

First, it is essential that the guide take charge and position clients with authority. But politely! If done right, this can be very frustrating, and keeping your cool can be hard. I have been out with guides who were cranky; their disposition ruined the day. And believe it or not, I've been accused of being a grouch myself, and I can tell you that I am better off sitting on the bank for a few minutes and cooling off than losing it. (When my client remarks how patient I am, this is usually a sign I'm about to explode and it's time to get away from the water!) Remember that rude is hell on tips.

When guiding two or three anglers in small creeks you might want to fish only one or two at a time. Doing this is even more judicious if the clients are interested in an "instructional" day.

Beginners and those accustomed to fishing busy places get fussy and love to dally around in one pool, and success is usually much greater if you can move them onward and cover more water.

You are not going on a regular fishing trip where everyone is on his or her own—you have to think of the consequences of the clients' actions—or inactions. And ask them kindly to be prepared and to go with the program. If they say they "don't need rain gear" and it rains, it is gonna be your ass getting wet—because you will be lending them your jacket. And if clients insist on fishing in those silly Teva things, you're the one who has to carry them home with a broken toe. Just as you will have to carry the camera bag, the rod tube, and maybe even the baby (as my son Nick had to do on one guiding trip. Because after the fish commenced to bite—parenthood be damned—it was, "Where can I put this baby?").

TEACH WITH INSTRUCTION AND EXAMPLE

Give casting instructions if you are qualified. If you are a self-taught caster who has never had professional casting lessons, you're probably not competent to teach.

Start the day by fishing for three or four minutes. That way you give the client a picture of what you will be trying to accomplish. Start in a honey hole where you can catch a fish, proving that fish are in the stream and that they can be caught.

Otherwise, don't fish except to demonstrate a point. Clients will never gripe about the guide fishing, but trust me, neither they nor their boss likes it. If it's been a long day, and the clients want to fish in the evening, it may be okay for you to fish—if you have already done a day's work and you have squared it with your clients. With the right clients it can be okay for you to fish the tough spots that they can't fish, but be careful: Your tip is pending. If asked to fish, go ahead, but don't go crazy and run off upstream. And try not to outfish the clients too badly. Remember: Your tip is pending.

Carry a rod and have it rigged with something different for different situations. And having another rod along—especially in rough country—is a good idea should the client break theirs.

When fishing more than one person, try to have the clients catch an equal number of fish.

The "expert" client is usually the tough one because he often thinks he doesn't need help. This is a very sensitive situation, so tread lightly because you don't want to bruise his ego. Make remarks such as "From my experience . . ." or "Last week when we fished this pool we stood just here and caught a huge one."

As part of my guides school we have lectures by my two most seasoned guides, Christoph Engle and Brian Spilman. They have different styles, but one thing they share is a lot of time midcurrent. Christoph guides almost a hundred trips a year and fishes nearly a hundred more. But every morning he asks the other guides their opinions about the fishing.

Brian Spilman does what it takes to catch fish—be it long hours or long hikes. Last summer he got seven C-notes in a row for tips! We don't

Guide Brian Spilman poses with a happy client.

know what exactly he does to get such great tips, but he is very fond of the phrase "I see." And "let me get that for you."

LUNCH

Lunch is an all-important time. It provides a good excuse to get away and reorganize. One of the main problems with lunchtime is that it often coincides with the best fishing. So carry a snack and eat late if that is advantageous because fishing often dies by 3 or 4 p.m.

Being a good fisherman is certainly an important part of being a good guide, but common sense, good manners, and an ability to teach are as important. Be honest about your experience—well, fairly honest—and if you find yourself getting frantic and obsessed, try to remember what I tend to forget: "It's just fishing."

ETIQUETTE

When you get on a few years as I have, "streamside manners" become less of an issue than when you were younger. If I find people fishing in the place I had planned to go, I walk over the hill and look for birds. (Birds live longer than other animals their size 'cause they fly away from stress!) This ability to avoid people whom you don't want to see—who include all fishermen seen out of doors—is a talent fully developed only in one's later years.

The me who does the guiding is dreadfully aware of the impact of others fishing "my water." (Another good description of "my water" follows shortly.)

I just fished at Lee's Ferry on the Colorado River in Arizona, and the river level was very high. There were about a dozen really good places to fish and about thirteen guides working that day. I learned a guide move that I hadn't seen before, namely the "grizzly charge." This occurred when we pulled in with our boat upstream a quarter-mile from a guide who was on the job. As we approached he suddenly burst toward us in a threatening manner, and although we couldn't hear much over our motor, his teeth were probably snapping. Deep water halted his advance, or else he might have bitten a hole in our boat (we lacked pepper spray or a pistola). Later that day another guide told us that if we ran into any guide on the river, that guide had "all water from there to the dam."

I always feel guilty floating a river, going by a wading fisher, and spooking her fish. I alleviate my guilt with a friendly jest or declare that she has "done better than us." Just the other day I told some bait fishers whom we were drifting by that someone was "catching a bunch of stockers" at a spot upstream (which was true).

Stream etiquette is just commonsense manners: You don't litter, you bury your crap, and you walk way around other fishers—because many people are there to be alone. (But say hello if you can't avoid them.)

And please pick up discarded line when you see it lying around. The birds get tangled up in it, and when you get old and your fishing hole is crowded, you are going to need those birds.

22

Fighting Fish

After watching people fight thousands of fish each year, you get an idea of why some land them—and why some don't. I can't do much to prepare people for fighting big fish. Sure, I can tie an old boot onto their line and throw it into moving water to illustrate the mechanics of fighting fish, but that still doesn't address the main problem.

STAY CALM

That problem is that anglers lose their cool. Often an angler doesn't have any cool to begin with and breaks off his prize when its instantaneous run triggers the fisherman's not-so-instantaneous response. At this critical point, the angler might freeze and clamp down on the line, heave, trip over his own feet, fall, flounder, scream, and, sadly in extreme cases

When fighting a fish, try to keep your cool, no matter how large that trout may be.

of great-size trout, get hauled in and drown. The size of the fish that causes such a state of insanity varies from one angler to the next. The beginning fly fisher may come apart with any size fish, but it may take a trophy of dangerous proportions to unnerve a seasoned angler. Rest assured that no matter how cool the customer, there's a fish out there that will rattle him. It's why we fish, isn't it?

Delightfully, the best way to learn how to overcome this affliction is by getting into the ring and duking it out with the lunkers. A bruiser at the other end of the line gets a lot more attention than an old boot, and the learning curve is steep when the stakes are high. Just one day with a good guide on a river like New Mexico's San Juan or central Oregon's Deschutes, for example, will teach you a great deal about fighting big trout.

PREPARE FOR THE BIG FISH

You can do a few simple things to prepare for hooking and fighting Mr. or Mrs. Big.

When in large trout territory, always use fluorocarbon tippet, check leaders for abrasions, and never, never leave wind knots in there because they decrease the strength of your leader by half. If you check for wind knots often, you may be able to undo them before they become too tight to untie. After they become that tight, the leader is compromised, and you should cut off and replace the tippet.

Check to make sure that hooks are sharp and not bent. If a hook is out of shape, don't try to bend it back. Discard and replace the fly.

Before fishing a likely spot, examine the proposed battleground in case you should hook "the Big." Be aware of snags, routes downstream, and places to beach a monster.

Don't fish with excess line hanging out of your reel. Use just the amount you need so you won't have a lot of slack to deal with if you hook a big one. Loose line has a habit of wandering around rod butts, reel handles, and other appendages.

USE YOUR DRAG

Oddly, there are people who have "opinions" about the drag on a fly reel, and I was once asked if it is legal to use the drag. And someone else told me that when he was a boy his father would forbid him to fish for the rest of the day if the father saw the son using the drag!

Barring moral objections to using the reel's drag, after the fish is on, it is important to get it under the control of your *quality* reel's drag system. This is a critical point in the fight. If you loop the line between the middle and fourth fingers, you can keep tension on each end while reeling in. Doing this gives you a loop that can be watched and maneuvered as line is reeled in. This process does, however, require dexterity with the fingers and is a tough operation for the inexperienced fly fisher to perform. Often a fish will be accommodating by running off with all the slack. You can augment this action, if you have done your scouting and know what's behind you, by backing up. If you start at midstream, back up onto the bank and in a position such that you can follow the fish downstream. If you reach the shore with the fish on the reel, you've won half the battle. From the bank you will have greater mobility as well as a height advantage. If one side of the stream has obstructions that the fish might tangle in, get onto the other side so you can steer the fish away from the trouble.

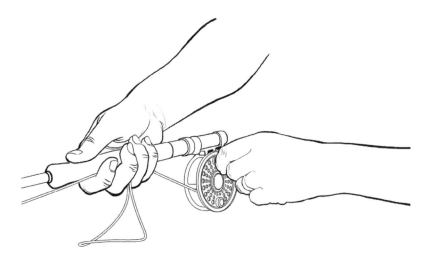

Placing the line between the middle and fourth fingers allows good control, but this is a dangerous time. Get your fingers away from the line ASAP when hooked to a lunker, and then trust in the drag.

When a big fish takes off, keep the rod tip high. This position keeps the angle of the line as vertical as possible, and that angle keeps fish or flies from fouling on a rock.

If you tend to break fish off just after they strike, you may not be getting your finger off the line fast enough after setting the hook.

Fish break off when screaming reel handles come into contact with clothes and hands, so keep the reel out away from your body. If your reel has a good drag, don't even touch it until it's time to wind line in.

When a good fish is hooked, anglers are often too cavalier. Focus on the fight. Stay on top of the fish and keep your arms way up in the air. Doing this is more important than people realize because it keeps the angle of the line as vertical as possible so there is less chance of its getting fouled on the bottom.

THERE'S A PLACE FOR BRUTE STRENGTH
When a fish heads for a snag, you may have to apply real muscle to turn it.

Anglers give too much credit to a fish by thinking it heads for a snag so that it can wrap the leader around it. The creature is merely scared to death and looking for a hiding place. For mathematical reasons beyond

A fly rod has a lot of power when held to the side. If a fish tries to run to the right, hold your rod sideways to the left and vice versa.

After you have the trout's head at the surface, net a big fish by leading it into your big net.

my understanding, a fly rod has much more power held sideways than overhead. To steer a fish, turn the rod in the direction opposite that in which the fish is swimming. If the fish is going right, the rod should be horizontal and on your left side.

In Jack Samson's wonderful biography, *Lee Wulff*, Lee talks about landing large fish quickly. "If you can convince them that they don't have a chance they will give up a lot sooner." You do this by getting the jump on 'em and using maximum pressure from the start. But only experience teaches you how much that is. Furthermore, although guides go nuts to see fish fought forever, beginners should go easy if conditions allow.

I have seen a multitude of fish lost because the fisher had no idea how much heat to apply. You can put a lot of steady pressure on monofilament. The sudden stresses are what "pop" the line.

KEEP YOUR DISTANCE — BUT KEEP UP

It is often best to fight fish from a distance so that there is plenty of forgiving stretch available in the line and leader. And keep some distance between you and a green fish because the fish may freak when it sees you at close range, make a wild dash, and break off.

A fly may pull out or break off if a heavy fish gets into the current and you don't follow it downriver fast enough. Always try to stay abreast of a large fish in a strong current so that you are not fighting it and the current, too. The fish's weight is greatly increased by the added force of the current.

CONCLUDING THE FIGHT

After the quarry has grown tired, you need to get its head above water and keep it there. This is when you finally have control, so don't ease up. Keep the fish coming at you and try not to let it get its head back under the surface. With its head above water, it can either be beached or netted.

Beaching a large fish works well if gravel bars or gently sloping shores are nearby. If the banks are steep or if you are in the middle of a large river, a net will save you many fish.

When a trout heads downriver, keep up with it!

NETS

While attending the Fly Tackle Dealer Show I noticed that the fad of long, narrow nets seems to be fading. That's good news for the fish because these "catch-and-release" nets aren't as environmentally sound as their manufacturers suggest. By the time you fit, fuss, and finagle a trout into one of them, the fish might die of old age. Carry the biggest net that you can and be sure that it has a wide front rim. And to protect a trout's delicate body, use a net made from the new rubberized material. The material is transparent, and because the fish can see through it, they are more willing to enter it.

And one last, important tip: *Don't go for the net too soon.* Wait until the fish is worn out and close enough that you don't need to reel anymore. If you get net in hand too early, it is going to occupy a hand that you need for other chores.

Wading

The most successful fly fishers work hard at getting close to the water they want to fish. Whether the objective is getting to a turbulent spot in the middle of a crashing river or slipping toward a riser in a quiet pool, wading is an important part of trout fishing.

DRESS RIGHT

For most rivers you need chest waders. Although many times it would seem that hip boots are sufficient for a small stream, we have found that when our guiding clients are in hippers they go home wet about half the time, either from going over the top or inadvertently sitting in the river.

Wading Shoes

The verdict seems to be in on felt soles, and there's little doubt that they are contributing to the spread of unwanted microscopic varmints in our waters. Although this horse is already well out of the barn, some states may have outlawed their use, so be careful that you aren't breaking the law just by stepping into the water with them on. But no matter what the manufacturer tells you, rubber-bottomed boots just don't stick as well as felt. The best alternative is rubber soles with spikes. Get shoes you can screw spikes into and out of so that you can remove the spikes when you are in a boat. Spiked shoes are unpopular with boatmen because they are tough on most boats' floors.

Having two pair is even mo' better. After you start using spikes, it is best to stay with them. Because when you get used to traveling on moss-covered rock with spikes, you are gonna bust your ass without them. Spikes are great for ice and slick grassy banks but do slide on dry rocks. Rubber soles, without spikes, are best for *dry* rocks.

Yes, we are gonna miss felt, but good riddance to it when you're walking on snow when the temperature is below freezing. If you have never had the pleasure, layer after layer of snow freezes to your feet, and you get an inch taller every step—until you topple over.

If you have a roof rack on your car, put your wading shoes there because they won't stink and dampen the inside of the vehicle. The ride outside will dry them faster and help to kill any germs hiding in them.

Frozen wading shoes, or old ones that have become very dry, are tough to put on in the morning. If the temperatures are expected to dip below freezing overnight, take your wet shoes inside. If you have old, ratty leather wading shoes, soak them before you try putting them on.

Try using shoe trees inside your wading shoes to keep them from shrinking. Buy your wading shoes on the *big* side anyway because you can fill in the extra space with socks that will warm and protect your feet.

Gore-Tex breathable waders are marvelous, neoprenes are okay for cold water, but breathable waders with sufficient undergarments are best. When the weather is warm, but not hot, I like to wear the Gore-Tex with nothing underneath. Many fly fishers I guide insist upon wearing waders on hot days when they would be better off without them. Often during summer I hear, at the end of a long hike, "I'm hot. I wish I had taken your advice and waded wet." The main drawback of getting wet is getting cold, so bring extra clothes in case the weather changes. Wear neoprene socks, quick-drying pants, and no underwear (like jeans, underwear takes forever to dry).

I fish a lot of clients who don't use gravel guards, or gaiters, over their waders. These accoutrements keep gravel out of shoes. Getting gravel in your shoes causes holes to wear in the wader feet and makes for uncomfortable walking at the least. Gravel guards also keep shoelaces from coming undone and prohibit flies and line from getting tangled in the laces.

STAFF UP

Wading staffs are handy tools, although they can get in the way while fishing. Collapsible ones seem to be best because they can be stashed out of the way when not in use. The low-budget angler can go to a ski slope (or ski shop) and find a lonely ski pole that has lost its mate, then turn it into a wading staff by simply tying a string to it. You can cut the cup off the bottom if you like, but leave it on if you typically wade in silted water. But metal staffs make an unnatural sound when they strike a rock, so slap some duct tape or something soft onto the end. I don't carry a staff per se, but when I have a hairy crossing to make, I hunt one up on the way to the river. When I've made my crossing, I leave it on the bank for the trip back.

TIPS FOR TROUBLED WATERS

Here is one little trick that has saved me many a dunking. When in a hairy spot, tottering and about to go for a swim, slap your rod into the river and use its leverage against the current to stabilize yourself. You can put your rod into the river to keep your balance well before you get into trouble. I'm not suggesting you use the rod as a wading staff. Don't touch the bottom with it; just hold it in the current. I must admit,

Sticking your rod into the water can help you maintain your balance while wading. Use a subtler form of this strategy when trying to wade slowly in quiet waters— just stick the rod tip barely in, and it will help you balance. *Nick Streit*

When wading treacherous water, linking arms with a companion can help prevent a spill. Always have the strongest wader/larger person on the upstream side.

however, that I have stuck the butt end onto the bottom and used it as a staff in emergencies.

Always wade facing upstream and never cross your legs. Don't let fear get the best of you. If panic tells you to dash for safety, stay put. Take a few deep breaths and continue slowly. Always wade slowly when in a tough spot.

When wading treacherous water with other people, link arms or place your arms around each other's shoulders or waist.

Rest assured that when your guide suggests such a union, he or she is not getting fresh but rather is just trying to keep everybody dry.

STEALTH IS IMPORTANT

Wading quietly, without pushing a wake ahead of you, can be very important in many types of fly fishing. Wade slower shallow water quietly because all fish are spooky in skinny water. An added problem occurs in streams with loose rocks. This is a real concern in Argentina because most rivers there run over softball-size round rocks that roll easily. When those rocks clink together, fish split the scene. The secret to quiet wading is taking smooth, even steps as you walk through the water. Avoid splashes or abrupt movements. Furthermore, don't false-cast while wading delicate water; doing that creates disturbances, too. Don't fight the current unless you have to, and when making a crossing, start as far upstream as possible and angle downriver with the flow.

Gear

Modern fishing vests have too many pockets, allowing people to carry a lot more than they need and causing them to fish around more in their vests than in the water. Treat your supplies as a backpacker would: When in doubt, leave it out.

CLOSE TO THE VEST

I have clients who fish far less than I do, but they carry a lot more gear than a professional guide. This is what I carry: flies, floatant, tippet, leaders, weight, strike indicators, nippers, tiny Swiss Army knife (featuring scissors), needle-nose pliers, and a catch-and-release tool. Those are the fishing-related items.

Then there are the nonfishing-related items, which vary with conditions and locale: lighter, sunscreen, spare lip gloss, tiny flashlight with extra batteries, adhesive bandages, a flat of duct tape, superglue, and drinking water.

Some optional items are a tape measure, binoculars, camera, and net.

All my guides use a lanyard around their neck for tippet and tools. These handy devices were invented by a guy who used to come into my shop with them thirty years ago. His name was Jerry Derryberry. Thanks for coming up with such a groovy gizmo, Jerry—wherever you are!

WHAT'S YOUR LINE?

Double-taper fly lines are better choices for most trout fishing than weight-forward lines because the thicker line of the DT feels better in the hands and doesn't tangle like the thinner WF lines will. For many trout-fishing situations, 30 or 40 feet is a very important distance. With a WF line you don't have enough line weight in the air to load the rod well. And you end up having to haul or shoot line, blowing your accuracy.

Fly rods are our most important tool. Make sure you choose one that's right for the job and right for your casting style. Try them out at your fly shop.
Nick Streit

MOST IMPORTANT TOOL

For many anglers, their love of fine fly rods is their undoing because they have too many rods and don't fish with them often enough to be familiar with each one's personality. If you're not a great caster, it may be better to get to know one good rod really well. Make it the right rod for the job. Light rods are great for small dry flies, but outsmarting trout is sufficient challenge without imposing the additional handicap of being undergunned.

Rods less than 8 feet in length may be best for small brushy creeks. But long rods mend and high stick better and let you reach out more efficiently—maneuvers needed for most all fishing. The long rod also allows you to drop (literally) the fly in tight quarters. When shopping for a rod, remember that a 9-foot rod must be high quality; a cheap 9-footer may carry a light price tag but be heavy. Of the new top-of-the-line models, the 4-weights are probably the best all-around trout rods and have replaced 5-weights for that category.

What kind of fly-rod action is best? Stiff rods tend to be accurate for short-yardage casts and mend well. They throw the tight loop necessary to slice through the wind, and that tight loop will slip a fly under the brush better than a softer rod. Stiff rods respond faster when a quick strike is needed when nymphing. Many anglers have a motion that is fast enough, but their rods react too slowly, and the fish spits the fly out. Furthermore, when you are fighting large trout a stiff rod will give you more control over the fish and tire it out quickly.

Soft rods are great for midrange fishing of 30 to 40 feet. They are also excellent when you are using small flies on light leaders, especially when big fish are the target. They are better for casting two flies or weighted flies with strike indicators because the wider loop that soft rods throw keeps things from tangling.

Catch-and-Release

Not only do catch-and-release regulations ensure a continued supply of big fish, but also they help maintain nature's balance. If trout aren't removed from the system, the equilibrium among food, space, and cover stays stable, thereby maximizing a river's potential and creating hungry fish and happy fishers.

I return fish for practical reasons: I'm not that crazy about eating them, and I need nice-size trout for my work. It's unfortunate that many modern fly fishers return fish and "fish only barbless" for lofty reasons. Catching fish and eating them are natural. Harassing them solely for our own amusement might be construed as selfish (interesting word, huh—*sel-fish*?). No doubt fish prefer torture over death, but personally I see no high moral ground onto which we catch-and-release anglers should climb.

HANDLE WITH CARE

If you are planning to release a trout, never put your fingers into its gills or lift it by hooking a finger under the gill plates. Instead, hold a trout, especially a large one, horizontally and upside down when it is out of the water. Not only does that position decrease its struggling, but also it is easier on its internal organs because fish aren't used to our brand of gravity.

To ensure that fish can be released in healthy condition, always play them for as short a time as possible. Therefore, use the heaviest tippet you can. Trout caught in warm-water lakes are much more susceptible to death from fishing than are those caught in moving water. River fish can nose up to white water to get oxygen, often in great concentrations, but stillwater fish aren't so fortunate. If a fish shows signs of succumbing, put it back into the water immediately and resuscitate it.

TROUT REVIVAL

Always revive a fish in calm water and place one finger into its mouth and grasp it gently above the tail. Then pull the fish back and forth slowly. Most people do this much too fast. Make the length of the stroke about equal to the length of the fish. Some fish may go into shock when released, especially in warm water, so release a weakened trout where it can be watched and recovered: in shallow water. Then, if it turns belly-up, you can retrieve it and attempt to revive it. If deep water prevents you from aiding a sick trout, try gently nudging it with your rod. This prodding is sometimes enough to bring it out of shock.

I have noticed that most anglers don't know when they should revive fish and often fool around with them unnecessarily.

Artificial respiration is seldom needed for trout being caught in fast, cold water. The released fish may appear a bit faint at first, but a few tumbles down the current will bring it around.

HOOK REMOVAL

When folks have a hard time getting the hook out of the fish, it is usually because they are holding the fly too close to the hook eye, and the hook merely pivots, or rocks back and forth. Whether you use forceps or fingers, grasp the hook at the very end of the shank, right above the bend. From that position it can be pushed straight back. Pushing it out is easier to do, of course, if the hook has been debarbed.

I find that a catch-and-release tool works very well on small trout, that is, fish light enough to be lifted by the leader. Apply the tool to the leader with your free hand anywhere above the fish, run it down onto the fly, give a little twist, and no more trout. By using the tool, you don't have to touch the fish or fly, saving wear and tear on both. The tool is far less useful for releasing larger fish because it needs to be put on a snug leader, and if a hefty fish is hanging on the leader, it will break.

My son Nick has learned that if you have a fish on the first fly of a two-fly rig—the hand fly—the fish will come off without your having to touch it if you take hold of the tail fly and pull. This can be done while the fish is still in the water—*if* the hand fly is tied in line and to the bend of the hook.

He also suggests that when a fish is hooked deep, or in the gills, it can be best to cut the line and let the trout swim away with the fly. The fish may function fine with it in there, or perhaps the fly will eventually rust or fall out.

BLOOD NEEDN'T SIGNAL FATAL INJURY

I used to think that all trout bleeding from the gills are bound to die and should be harvested, but recently, while fishing in a beaver pond, I caught a large brown that was bleeding badly from the gills. No way was I interested in lugging this 5-pound fish around, so I worked like an emergency-room doctor to revive it. And by God, in a few minutes the bleeding had stopped. I released the fish, and it was swimming around in the pond the following day. I don't know if the large size and vigorous health of the trout saved it, but since that experience I don't keep many injured fish.

Large hooks are more damaging than smaller ones to a trout.

Head guide Nick Streit on the Brazos River of New Mexico briefly holds a fish out of water for a photo. Note that the fish is also held close to the water so that if it falls, it doesn't land on the land.

PHOTOS SHOULD BE "SNAP" SHOTS

When taking photos of a fish that you plan to return to the water, be sure to make it a snappy photo. Hold the fish out of the water for only brief periods, or take your photos with the fish halfway in the water so that it is breathing water rather than air. Recent studies have shown that this method is a prime factor in survival rates.

Exploring for Trout

I live and guide close to one of the world's most popular fishing holes, New Mexico's San Juan River. I also spend a lot of time fishing the wild waters of Patagonia, Argentina. Even there, at the other end of the world, I am often asked about the fishing on the San Juan. The sound of big fish splashing carries a long way. When I tell the Argentine fly fishermen that the San Juan is too crowded for my tastes and that I haven't fished it in years, they say, "Just where do you fish in that desert, if you don't fish there?" There are plenty of other places to fish—you just have to look. I even wrote a book on the subject—albeit a thin one—*Fly Fishing New Mexico*.

Herd mentality and the allure of big fish send 90 percent of fly fishers to the 10 percent of water that everyone hears so much about. And on one of those popular big tailwaters river like the San Juan you can catch big fish, have fun, and learn a lot at the same time. Also, such waters are great for people who have little time because the trails to such places are well worn and easy to follow.

If you have fished there a lot you'll know in advance what fly to fish in which fashion. Remember, however, that most of these heavily fished places will have neurotic trout that will be selective and need to be fished for in a singular fashion. A guide, at least for your first day, is highly recommended.

But if you like being alone and are tired of civilized places, you may want a little adventure, exercise, and solitude with your fishing. Finding new water is an art unto itself. The good news is that plenty of such places exist. The bad news is that the trails to these spots are faint and poorly marked. Of course, if you love wild trout and the places in which they thrive, that's good news.

ASK QUESTIONS FIRST

Presume that no matter how remote a place seems, someone knows more about it than you do. I spent a lot of time exploring blue holes, chasing bonefish and snapper with my son Nick in the vast and remote interior of South Andros Island in the Bahamas. We'd go so far back into the bush that we'd say, "We must be the first men to ever fish this place." Later we talked the place up to someone in our confidence, and he said, "Oh yeah, mon, you mean where dat bush en' little blue hole is, wid all dem snappar."

Instead of wandering around blindly to find the place, we could have asked first and perhaps headed there in a much straighter line. We fisher folk, however, seem to have an inordinate amount of pride and are seldom direct. It's tough to swallow that lump of pride and ask questions. It's like rolling down the car window in a strange town and asking directions from others; sometimes they're wrong, but more often they're right on. Of course, getting directions to Wal-Mart is considerably easier than getting directions to somebody's honey hole, especially if the bearer of the information has nothing more to gain than seeing your ugly face at his favorite spot. Don't be surprised to hear that it's a long drive and a miserable hike and that rattlesnakes await your arrival. One of the best places I've ever fished had ingenious signs warning of radioactivity, obviously erected by some clever angler. At least I hope that's the case and that the ringing in my ears is from too much espresso.

However, consider the consequences before you ask certain people to show you their secret fishing spots. I have a couple of good fishing holes for which I sold my soul, vowing, "No, I won't take anyone, no, not even my children, here." So I'm lonely when I fish there. On occasion it can be better to go the extra distance and find such places on your own rather than be in debt the rest of your life.

Fly shops have good information, but it's of great value to them. Tight-lipped shopkeepers may irritate fly fishermen, but try putting yourself in their shoes, and maybe you'll understand their position. Remember that what's a passionate pastime to you is a living to them. Some guy who may be a cutthroat businessman at home arrives on the fishing scene and expects "free love" at water's edge. Not much is free these days, and I can tell you as a former fly-shop owner that the value of the information will generally rise with the value of goods purchased. Of course, everyone everywhere is different, and you might just walk into a shop and be given the map to old Walter's hideout.

Where fishing pressure is not an issue, free love may still be practiced. This unfortunately leaves out most of the continental United States.

GET A GUIDE

A good fly-fishing guide will take you to places that he knows well and that have predictable results. If you are looking for someplace wild and unfished, you might ask the guide if there is somewhere he has been meaning to explore and say that you would be willing to participate in the experiment. I love that kind of job because there is always some-place, or some stretch of a familiar river, that I want to check out but haven't. Of course, if I'm getting paid to go, that's fantastic. The client will be taking a gamble but will get to see how the guide goes about the exploration. Because he's bought a partnership for the day, he gets to share in the discovery.

GOVERNMENT SOURCES OF INFORMATION

Government agencies—game and fish departments and Bureau of Land Management and Forest Service offices—can be excellent sources of information and will have maps, regulations, and current road, weather, and water conditions. More important, they have on staff fisheries biologists who are, surprisingly, seldom quizzed by the public. Often these biologists don't fish for sport, so they will unhesitatingly tell you the truth. A fisheries biologist once told me about a nest of huge brown trout he had found.

"Yes, 3-pound brown trout are in a beaver pond up there," he said in a matter-of-fact manner, "but you have to walk a quarter-mile and cross two fences to get to them." It didn't mean much to him, and he just as well could have been telling me that he had found a rare subspecies of termite. Game wardens, too, can be a great source of information, being out in the field every day. Most view part of their job as helping people get their fish and game and are usually more than happy to be of service.

TREASURES CLOSE TO HOME

Those fishers who live in congested areas need not despair; good fishing may be closer—much closer—than you might think. Instead of looking for what would appear to be the choice sections of a creek, you may want to head the other way. Many of the best fishing—and hunting—places that I have found are ones that are simply overlooked because everyone assumes that they are overused. Even in the West, the best water can often be found where you would least expect it to be—next to houses, dumps, thrift stores, and other detractions. Let me put it this way: If there are two sections of an accessible stream, one idyllic, the other running by a gravel pit and under a stack of junk cars, try the dumpy spot.

If you are in the habit of driving by a piece of river or stream often, notice which sections get fished and how much pressure they seem to be receiving. Certain areas will receive much less pressure than others will. Perhaps the lack of parking areas or the presence of an unchained malamute keeps pressure down on a promising stretch of stream. Figure out how to access and fish some sweet little spot. Slide in and out of it like a thief in the night, using whatever it takes—disguises, lies, you name it. All's fair in love, war—and the whisper of fishing spots.

EXPLORE TIMES AS WELL AS PLACES

When planning a trip to a place where fishing pressure is an issue, it can be wise to fish weekdays and other times when others don't. Some of the best fishing in the West can be during the prerunoff in early spring. That's when the fish are starving, the trees are greening, and the caddis are hatching—but the anglers are still in hibernation!

KNOW WHAT YOU'RE LOOKING FOR

It is always nice to know what resides in the water you plan to fish. You can sometimes get fish-per-mile statistics from fly shops, fisheries biologists, or fishing friends. For the kind of wild water for which you may be looking, however, those numbers are probably unavailable. You will have to figure that out on your own.

I always feel excited when I step into new water, especially when that step coincides with the dining schedule of the stream's residents. I feel blessed then because from that feeding period I will have a fairly clear picture of the river's fish population. The fish don't even need to eat for very long. If they feed actively in one pool, I can guesstimate what is swimming around in the next one because if the next pool is similar to the one from which you caught fish, it should hold an equal number of trout. Obviously, the better you can read water, the more accurate the count will be. This research work is an advanced form of angling that is beyond catch-and-release. You get to count the fish you caught, the ones you missed, and even those you just saw; they all go into the equation.

GET AN OVERVIEW

I always try to see as much of a stream as possible on my first visit. That way I will know where the best water is for future trips. I'll do this by keeping an eye out for trout while walking briskly along the bank. If the fish are at all active, you should get to see quite a few of the rascals before they can dodge you. If you don't see any fish, don't despair. That doesn't mean there aren't any. It may mean simply that they aren't feeding and are lying up.

My favorite method of exploring a new stream is to use a combination of the aforementioned techniques. By fishing only the best holes and walking over the rest of the water, I not only get the exploring job done but also hopefully get to catch some nice trout while doing it.

IF BIG FISH ARE THE OBJECTIVE

Seemingly, the best places to fish are those with a high number of trout, but that is not always the case. Some of my favorite rivers don't hold many fish, but the trout are big. The low fish count keeps the fishing pressure down because when the average guy fishes it, he really doesn't know exactly where to fish and goes home skunked, never to return. We guides love that kind of stream because those lonely big ones are seldom bothered and may be gullible. If you fished only the places capable of holding big trout, you could have some very good sport.

Large trout, however, are efficient diners and seldom eat for long spells, especially when they have plenty of space and food. To catch the fish on the feed, you either need to do a lot of fishing until you hit the right time or know when conditions are perfect. The latter may be a combination of favorable water levels and temperatures, combined with the availability of big bugs like stoneflies or hoppers. Obviously this second option beats the hell out the first option of hours of fruitless fishing, so find out all you can. When everything looks right, go for it.

WHERE FISH ARE PLENTIFUL

At the other end of the scale, when fish numbers are so high that they push the carrying capacity of their environment, the fish will have to feed a lot. This feeding is often carried to the extreme on streams where nonnative species have been introduced because they seem to overpopulate more than the indigenous fish do.

This is the case with most rivers in the United States, spawning a new, ever-growing push to reestablish native species. Though this movement is pushed by Trout Unlimited and is well intentioned, idealism often overpowers good sense because much of the natives' home water is too silted and warm for them now. We are very fortunate to have the tougher nonnative trout that somewhat fill the ensuing gap. Unfortunately, here in New Mexico thousands of native Rio Grande cutthroats are stocked in waters where they simply don't survive.

POPULATIONS ARE DYNAMIC

The composition of a stream is dynamic, that is, always changing. It is possible to see the size, number, and even species change over time. One stream that I know of in Colorado used to swarm with small brook trout, but now, ten years later, it is inhabited solely by good-size browns.

ENVIRONMENTAL FACTORS AFFECT TROUT

Logging, grazing, development, and irrigation are important factors to consider when sizing up new water. Learning to understand what roles these factors play in your fishing will put you one rung up on the ladder toward being an expert angler and outdoorsman and serve you well in your pursuit of productive trout waters.

Irrigation

It's June in the Rockies—heaven on Earth—and you wade into a gorgeous piece of water that winds through rich, green farmland. Flycatchers flit out of the streamside alders to grab mayflies. The world is alive with life, and the fishing is good. The memory of the fishing and the beautiful river visit your waking and sleeping thoughts often over the next couple of months, but when you finally return you find not that lovely, healthy river but instead a skinny trickle of water that has been shrunk by thirsty farms.

When river levels drop like that, fish may head for cooler water above irrigation head gates or hunker down in the few remaining deep holes. The larger browns will hide under banks, roots, and trees. Those fish are virtually uncatchable in summer's low and warm water—during the daytime. They are, however, very catchable if you linger late into the evening. By "late" I mean when stars flicker in the sky and you need a flashlight to get back to the car.

When fishing such low water, hightail it from one hole to the next. Unlike higher water, when the fish can be anywhere, the low flow means that you will at least know where they are. This low-water condition will be exacerbated if there is considerable grazing along the river.

Overgrazing

Overgrazing has been a factor for so long that few really notice it. But it is huge, especially on smaller creeks in the West. I know of one stream with incredible trout numbers in its rocky, canyon stretch because the boulders aren't affected by the cattle's hooves and appetite. When the stream emerges from the canyon and heads into flat meadowlands, the trout population plummets. This is where the lazy bovine whiles away the day, all of his needs met at streamside. He munches the bright green grass on the bank and then, with a simple 180-degree maneuver, turns and hurls the brown remains into the river. Alas, this isn't even the cow's worst contribution. That "honor" belongs to its huge round hooves as they flatten and trample the stream bank. The munching and mashing of riparian vegetation by cattle drastically reduce the lush growth, causing terrestrial and aquatic insects to lose their homes and water temperatures to rise due to lack of shade. In warmer climes that are on the brink of modern trout range, such as the Gila wilderness in southwestern New Mexico, you will not find trout in streams where substantial grazing occurs.

On the bright side, more and more streams on both public and private land are being fenced to avoid this desecration. Ranchers are finding fencing to be in their best interest because when the area adjacent to the stream is fenced, the water table is higher, which is important in dry times.

Logging

Just as in places that are overgrazed, the defoliation of a watershed will cause the waters to rise and fall drastically. In an area with which I am familiar, only a couple of streams have never been logged or grazed. This, of course, not only makes them solid trout streams but also allows them to be studied in contrast with the more average, abused watersheds. The most glaring contrast can be seen during runoff, when the logged streams are over their banks with brown water, whereas the pristine watersheds run full but clear. Because the pristine creeks are not grazed, the root structure of the native plants holds the banks together. The banks of the abused creeks crumble, washing downriver with each flood.

The healthy stream's runoff will last well into summer and maintain a good flow until snowfall. When I hear about another horrible flood somewhere, I am always amazed that the reasons why these catastrophes happen constantly are so seldom mentioned.

Mining

Contrary to what spokesmen for mining operations might say, mining has never been of any particular benefit to any watershed. I'm especially touchy on this subject, having lived through the demise of what was probably the richest trout stream that I have ever fished, the Red River in northern New Mexico. Twenty years ago this incredible little river regularly produced wild cutbows of 3 and 4 pounds. Large-scale mining of molybdenum by Unocal of California (now Chevron) killed those fish—and they have yet to return.

As I write this the Pebble Gold Mine in Alaska is destined to destroy way more of our Earth and its inhabitants—including lots of fish. Hopefully by the time you are reading this, that project will have been scrubbed in light of the great amount of pressure applied against it.

Global Warming

Humanity's reign on our world is obviously coming to a close. Not necessarily a bad thing because those of us who make it past the Mad Max business will have a lot of water to fish—even if it is perhaps lifeless. The current effects of global warming include the well-publicized symptoms of increased temps and rowdy storms, but there are less-publicized symptoms, such as the amount of dust accumulating on top of the snowpack in the San Juan Mountains of the southern Rockies each spring after violent windstorms. The darkened snow melts fast and runs off in a destructive rush, resulting soon in a parched river.

In the Southwest where there is a lot of loose soil, we have had such intense downpours that flash floods have been literally changing the structure of rivers. Just a few years ago that same beleaguered Red River in northern New Mexico had two separate one hundred-year floods *in one month* that wiped out all the trout there. (Thankfully, the stream rebounded in about two years.)

GUIDEBOOKS

A lot of fishing guidebooks cover various states and regions. Those that aren't very wordy are probably of more value afield than are the thicker ones. As the author of one, I can safely say that you won't find everywhere in them. When reading guidebooks or magazine articles, keep in mind that not all is revealed—or known. When I wrote my guidebook I struggled over whether to include a number of places. I wanted to be both responsible to the places and to readers. Certainly you don't want to ruin water by drawing too much attention to it. I had learned this lesson the hard way when I wrote about a sweet little spot in another guidebook some years ago. That book became popular and may have contributed to the considerable increase in fishing pressure on that once-peaceful stream. Also bear in mind that some spots are unknown to the writer, others are too delicate and small to reveal, and yet others are spoken of only in whispers.

DO HOMEWORK FOR LAKE EXPLORATION

When exploring lakes, place considerable emphasis on homework. Because most trout lakes in the West don't support natural reproduction and instead rely on stocking, much can be learned from fisheries biologists. Ask about winterkill and food. Many high-elevation lakes serve trout only skimpy meals—midges and terrestrials. If, however, you learn that there are freshwater shrimp and/or snails, grab your rod because fish get big on that grub.

FIELDWORK

Let's get outside where a fisher is supposed to be. We'll be armed, of course, with the proper research equipment—waders, rods, flies, and so on.

I write this overlooking the Quilquihue River in Argentina. I'm again involved in the painstaking work of finding good fishing for my clients. Just below my window the fish are small, but I'm hoping that with a hike downriver and away from the road, I'll find fish that grow larger.

I walk some forty dusty minutes and slide down the steep bank and wade out into the river. I cast indiscriminately in some fast water because I believe there will be monsters everywhere. I do catch a small rainbow, but he's not what I had in mind. So I go upstream in search of better water. This river is new to me, so I should be fishing only spots in which I have confidence. The water and the sky are both very clear, so I'll fish fast and only at the heads of the pools. The fish will be easier to fool there, and that is usually where the feeding fish will be. I will fish only these really good spots because, after all, I've got a lot of river to myself.

In doing this scouting I pay great attention to sign on the banks. Is there a trail, and is it well used? If there are many footprints, I hope they are tracks of felt soles because that would indicate catch-and-release fishermen. I come across a most gruesome find, a recent camp where

A hidden jewel in the southern Rockies. Scouting, indeed, can pay off.

fish have been grilled on a spit. That's like finding the fox's tracks on the way into the henhouse.

WHEN'S DINNER?

I also investigate streamside how much food is available and at what time of year or day a particular place will fish best. The food factor is fairly simple. I look under the rocks out from the water's edge and note the insects and their abundance. If I find a lot of stonefly nymphs, I'll be there in early summer for the hatch. If I am looking in the spring and see grass starting to grow streamside, I know that I may be fishing on hoppers later in the summer.

What time of day will the particular body of water fish best? Streams that flow west may fish best late in the day, when the sun is at your back. This is especially true on a small stream where trout tend to be wild and spooky. Such fish can see you coming from a long way off if they have the sun in their favor. Whenever possible, in any fishing situation, it is wise to have the sun behind you. You will have a better view of the fish, your fly, and the bottom.

A FINAL HINT

When you find that dream spot where big trout lazily drift up to inhale dry flies, the tough part is not bragging about it. From considerable and painful experience I can assure you that it won't be as important a secret to the next person you tell. Its confidentiality becomes less and less honored as it gets blabbed about down the line, and before you know it the place will be overrun. You'll hate yourself for ever opening your mouth to anyone about it. If you have to brag, do what I do: lie.

Maps

You can learn a lot about proposed fishing spots by studying maps. If you are looking for out-of-the-way water, start your search with state highway maps. Here you can get the big picture, which may be far more important than you might think. Because the kind of water we're looking for is probably not close to any big cities, slide your finger across the highway map until it settles where the roads turn thin and wavy. Then, when you know the general area you want to fish, switch to government maps. Forest Service or Bureau of Land Management maps don't give you the lay of the land, that is, the topography, but they will reveal land ownership.

Topographic maps are the final step. They can be found at bookstores, outdoor stores, and some fly shops (ours!). They can be purchased from afar by writing to Map Branch of Distribution, U.S. Geological Survey, P.O. Box 25286, M.S.-306, Denver, CO 80225. For information, you can phone (303) 202-4700. Maps to be printed out can also be bought online. If you are doing your trout studies by computer, visit www.usgs.gov. Another excellent website is www.map quest.com. Our friend John Wilson puts Google Earth and topo maps on his computer screen at the same time—yes, he is a computer genius for an older cat. Doing this gives him the complete story on places he plans to hunt and fish.

Besides revealing the roads, trails, and topography, careful study can tell you much more. For instance, in small mountain streams, the flatter, open areas are where large beaver dams might be found. If you take that one step further, look for nearby springs or small tributaries. Dams in main channels generally wash out during runoff, but the dams on smaller feeder creeks and springs may stay intact for years, long enough to grow large trout.

In beaver country you never know when the investigation into such little brooks will pay off. I once spied a creek that looked especially promising because it had aquatic plants. Such vegetation—especially watercress—may signify that the stream is spring fed, and spring creeks are rich. I hiked up the foot-wide creek for about a mile until I came to the Hoover Dam of beaver dams. It closed off a small canyon and stood about 15 feet high. The aspen logs that comprised the dam were all old and gray, so I knew that the dam had been there long enough to grow big fish. The spring poured out of the earth just above the pond, giving it a rich and stable water supply, unaffected by the floods of the nearby river. I ascended a little hill to have a look down into the pond. From this height I could see into the clear water perfectly and saw what was to become the biggest trout that I have ever caught in the United States. It actually took me three years to catch Wally, as I came to call him; the story is in my book *Man vs. Fish: The Fly Fisherman's Eternal Struggle*.

Whether checking maps of large or small rivers, pay attention to the "snakier" sections because bends create deep pools. Also look for areas where tributaries and side canyons join a river because they add character, in the form of boulders, rocks, and wood, to the main flow.

Topo maps also reveal whether you are looking at meadow or forest. Open areas are white, and timbered country is green. This information can be of help in the hunt for user-friendly high lakes to fish in the West. Bring a lot of flies to the lakes surrounded with green because the trees will probably end up wearing many of them. Besides looking for treeless banks to fish, look for level shorelines where the contour lines are far apart because those shores will probably ease off into the shallow, wadable water that feeding fish like. Contrary to popular belief, on lake and stream, the shallower water produces the most life—and best fishing.

If your interest lies in finding the most-remote and least-fished water, study topo maps for areas that lie beyond canyon walls, mountains, and other nuisances. Always bear in mind two facts: People love to catch and eat fish but are basically lazy, and the amount of fishing pressure that a particular piece of water gets is usually in inverse proportion to the effort required in getting there.

But that statement needs to be qualified: Twenty years ago if you hiked a distance into the backcountry, you could be fairly sure you would be alone. Today, however, some areas of the United States (Colorado) are filled with vigorous people who think nothing of hiking 5 miles for a day's fishing. So if you are headed up a trail, and what looks like the Olympic cross-country fly-fishing team sweeps past you, don't hesitate to change your plans and fish closer to the car. In some places, you may actually find less fishing pressure there than at the end of the trail.

Drift Boat Fishing

My son Nick bought a nice inflatable boat for us to guide out of this year. We basically have only one section of the Rio Grande to use it on, and I have always been reluctant to go to the trouble of floating the water because it is flanked by a good road. I had thought that we were fishing it pretty thoroughly, but I was wrong because we have discovered that floating this same section of water finds one's fly in good water much more often than when on foot. And nooks and crannies that we had somehow never fished—or even known about—have become accessible.

On many rivers the good spots are just too far apart for foot travel, or the river is too big and fast to wade. In such a case, floating can be a fast-paced and exciting way to fly fish rivers. On a moderately paced river, an average float will cover 8 miles. Voyages any longer than that will allow little time to dally or wade fish. Various state navigation laws often allow trespass through private property by boat and not by foot. Floating is indeed the way to go if restricted by age, condition, or disposition.

When booking a float trip be sure to get a proper fly-fishing guide because a "river guide" will have not a clue what to do with you. (Ask what kind of boat you would be fishing from—rafts and inflatables need to have fishing frames.) A good fly-fishing guide knows not only how to row the river but also how to catch its fish. He or she is responsible for your safety and comfort and can even control a fly's float. He may even give the oars a little tug at just the right moment to help you set your hook! That's a good guide. A great guide will make you think that you were the one responsible for catching the fish.

Having the fly close to the bank is usually the goal on most rivers, and a good boatman will maneuver you into casting range for your skills—or lack thereof. It is often necessary to ask your oarsman to get

You'll catch more fish by keeping your fly in the water. When drifting through a prime stretch, raise and lower the rod instead of making time-consuming casts.

close in so that you can reach the good water. If fishing a dry or a dry/ dropper, it is advisable to make a reach cast that places fly, leader, and line in the same current.

One of the hardest things to get used to in float fishing, if you are in the bow of the boat, is casting far enough ahead—downstream—so that your partner in the back (stern) has water to fish. The problem here is that your attention—from the bow—doesn't naturally fall to where your next cast should be because you are watching your fly as it drifts adjacent to the boat. The bow angler needs to force himself to look well ahead. A good guide will remind the bow fisher to cast well downstream.

REFLOATING THE FLY

When you are wade fishing you can daydream, rest, or look at the birds. When you wake up, you'll be in the same spot. When you are float fishing quick rivers, however, each false cast you make takes your fly out of the water and past another likely spot. You can get your fly more playing time on the water by refloating it rather than casting. When the fly's drift has been exhausted, it will be below the boat and starting to drag. Lift the rod to vertical—or past vertical—and then maneuver the line this way or that upstream of where you think a fish is. Lower the rod, and the fly can be fished again for a few feet.

CAMP FLOATS

Unlike day-long floats with lots of waiting and shuttles, camp floats allow one to luxuriate in the trip—you put your waders on early in the morning and fish until dark if you like. Or you can kick back and put your feet up as you quietly drift through nature. Just as you do with any type of camping, you don't want to go for just one night (because it took three days to pack). So arrange for two or three nights. Too bad there aren't more rivers to do this on, but it is a common way to fish Alaska and rivers in the northern Rockies, Argentina, and Chile.

RODS

Ask the guide if it's possible to take two or three rigged rods. On a normal float there will be good streamer, nymph, and dry-fly water. (And broken rods are so common in boats that having an extra is important, too.)

The Traveling Angler

We are often baffled at the fly shop by people's choices of where and when they fish. That's because traveling anglers often lack reliable information. Directions may come from businesses that have a horse in the race or from fellow fishers as rumors. That hasn't changed all that much since Isaac Walton outstretched his arms—"It was *this* big"—and then pointed thataway.

GOOD AND BAD INFORMATION

It's important to remember, though, that despite the high-falutin' talk, fly fishing is an ego-driven pursuit and can bring the braggart out in us all. The old maxim "all fishermen are liars" doesn't exclude fly fishers. This is especially true when it comes to fly-fishing publications or television shows that we get so much info from. All that is often required for a guy to style himself an expert is a pen or a camera and a current fishing license. And those with deep pockets—but no real qualifications—simply want to be in the fishing business and to broadcast their personal fish stories on TV.

Even if the information you receive from these sources is correct, it is common for the overeager angler to wade into the right water but *at the wrong time.* We have learned in the fly shop that we can't talk sense into such love-struck anglers and just sell them the flies they have on their list and wish them "good luck." (This fly list is often contrived by someone who fished the place once for the story.) When they come back to the shop the next day skunked, they are pliable, and we can direct them to better fishing.

Aside from a couple of honest magazines and websites, most of what you find these days will be fish porn. Guidebooks are likely the most accurate because a publisher has to take the risk of putting the book out, so the writer usually has credibility. But beware of guidebooks based only on the author's best days on particular water. If it sounds too good to be true, . . . you know the rest.

There are many fishing reports online and in newspapers, and they may be accurate, but even the best of them describe what *already happened* and not what is about to happen. Fly shops and guides keep up on their local conditions and should know what is *fixin' to happen*—so that we are standing on the bank when it does. By the time the crowds get the published reports, our clients have already caught 'em all! When you call fly shops, first ask if they are busy so that you don't end up with a rushed response.

If you are interested in fishing in another area entirely, and you have someone you trust in the fly-fishing business, ask that person whom to contact. Those of us in this relatively small business know who the straight shooters are and where the really good fishing usually is.

Fly-fishing clubs and anglers groups often publish members' fishy findings, but many contributors may be better at casting blame about a fishing trip than at casting a fly. I once took a guy fishing, and we had what I thought was good action—skating dry flies to 14–16-inch trout. But when I read this gentleman's article it didn't sound like he was as delighted with the fishing—and oddly there was no mention of his missing all those strikes! (We guides also count the fish that *eat* the fly—along with those that get caught.)

THE STATES

Due to the sheer amount of fly fishing in the United States, it can be an overwhelming task to figure out where to go. But doing the homework can be fun in itself. Still, be aware that the places that get the most attention in print get the most pressure, too. Look around the edges of the big-name rivers. The ones in Montana have many fishermen, whereas the state you will probably be driving through in order to get there—Wyoming—gets largely ignored and has fabulous fishing in its own right. Colorado gets a lot of play and rightly so because there is a crazy amount of fishing there. At my brother Jackson's fly shop, the Mountain Angler in Breckenridge, the guides do dozens of trips a day in summer. They all gotta catch fish, and to accomplish this magical feat, they go to private water, technical water, beginner water, floating water—Colorado's got it all.

Lesser-known places to fish, like New Mexico and Utah, may not have the *quantity* of streams that draws the crowds, but that doesn't mean the *quality* isn't there. And if isolation and beauty are important to your happiness, check out these states.

The famous tailwaters of the West will get you big fish with relatively little physical effort. They tend to be geographically isolated, but because they are well known for offering some of the best trout fishing in the world, you will be sharing the river with many others. So the fish get fussy, and being surrounded by trout but not catching any can be frustrating. But with the normal preponderance of small insects in tailwaters, the fish have to eat a lot of them. Guides will know how to catch the fish, although it is virtually impossible for a visiting angler to do well without help initially.

Sometimes the fish can be fooled by what is usually overlooked—simplicity. Last year I went to fish the Taylor River in Colorado, and I had heard that the only way to catch the fish was on a standard deep nymph rig with a shrimp pattern rigged precisely so. But when I arrived in late morning there were a few big stoneflies hatching, and I had been told in the Dragon Fly Shop in Crested Butte that fish could be caught on the adult stone. I saw the hefty splash of a trout eating a big meal and proceeded to hook the fish on my first cast with a huge fly. I hadn't even put on my waders, and I had to run down the bank and displace all the nymph fishermen in order to fight the 6-pound fish. I didn't see anyone else catch a trout for hours on nymphs. And it can be dreary work to dredge these tailwaters all day!

Fishing the off-seasons—late autumn to early spring—is a good idea. One winter I went to fish the San Juan here in New Mexico to get information for my book *Fly Fishing New Mexico*. Having an open calendar, I studied the weather forecast and planned to arrive during a patch of relatively warm and windless weather. I caught a lot of trout by being rowed downriver by great guides: Curtis Bailey, John Tavner, and Rick Hooley. Winter trout often do a good deal of their feeding on top as midges assemble in the afternoon, and we drifted to different groups of risers that the guys knew about. There were even a few may-flies (BWOs) in the warmest part of the day.

The eastern United States has endless miles of trout streams. I was raised fishing the fabled Beaverkill and Ausable Rivers, although it didn't take me long after moving to the West to become a Rocky Mountain snob (not to be confused with a Montana snob, who is at a yet-higher level). But on a recent trip to the East I rediscovered the good trout fishing of New York State—on the Batten Kill. There is some really interesting fishing tucked away in surprisingly remote locales on that river. Pressure seemed not that much more than on western streams (which, we snobs must admit, have become way busier than they were a couple of decades ago). The western reaches of New York also have some extremely large trout during spawning runs from the Finger and Great Lakes.

When looking for the greatest numbers of big trout—and other salmonids—in the fifty states, Alaska is, of course, tops. Keep in mind that it is a long ways off, tough to get to, and expensive. The weather is fussy, and the bugs pesky, but the wildness is the greatest on Earth. The rainbows will not be fussy, however, if you give them eggs and meat flies. If you are a classic kind of trout fisher who prefers your trout on dry flies, head elsewhere.

INTERNATIONAL FLY FISHING

I have twenty years in the international fly-fishing business—bonefishing in the Bahamas and then trout fishing in the Argentine. Saltwater fly fishing is the tougher of the two because flats fishing is all about seeing fish. You have to the have proper lighting conditions, and then, after the fish are sighted, a good cast needs to be delivered. For my own recre-ational fishing I would hit the flats only when the weather and sea were calm and clear. And with living right on the water, that was only about once a week in winter.

The trout-fishing business is less stressful because you can always catch some form of the numerous fishes, no matter the clients' abilities or conditions. And there is something about the surroundings in trout fishing that elicits serenity in client attitudes. The pursuers of seafaring fish, on the other hand, set their jaws hard and are far more serious: There are slams, mini slams, and grand slams.

The great draw of going to the opposite end of the world—Argentina, Chile, and New Zealand—is that the fishing is prime when, in the northern latitudes, the quarry is hibernating. Although long-range plans are necessary, going when conditions are expected to be favorable is just as important as elsewhere.

An overriding factor—common to choosing virtually any fishing place—is human population density. If there are a lot of us hungry humans around, a percentage thereof will likely eat the trout (unless there are *enforced* catch-and-release laws). In the book *Reeling in Russia*, Fen Montaigne's good writing kept me wading along with him as he fished across the country—from west to east. A dreary journey because Russia, despite being four times larger than the United States, is pretty well trashed by poachers. He didn't find good fishing until he ran out of civilization at Kamchatka. One phone conversation with an international fly-fishing professional would have saved the author thousands of miles of poor fishing—but admittedly would have nixed the premise of a good book.

As is the case with any loosely planned fishing trip, he had some hilariously bad guides. Guiding is a real profession in North America, but when you leave the States anyone can be a fishing guide. Some countries have licensing protocols, and in Argentina there are rigorous standards and tests for qualification as a *guia*. But official credentials don't mean much to a fish. Always ask to check references. (So that you can keep track of your loot, it is wise to deal with an agent in the States and make payments here.)

Booking Agencies
If you can afford it, you can always book an entire week with one of the many fly-fishing travel agents who do "canned" trips. These week-long affairs at lodges or *estancias* are the most common way to fish internationally. The fishing will be on proven water, and the excursions will be well orchestrated. These will be the most expensive, but

if you are not accustomed to foreign travel you will feel safe. And you will have your own stretch of water and—although the last explorer is probably just around the bend—you will feel like the first person to ever fish there.

Those with adventure in their soul are going to feel too insulated in this situation. And although language can be an issue, there is no reason why a foreign fisher can't do the same as one in the United States would—fish from a central location with different guides and outfitters. Doing this provides perhaps the best and most interesting fishing because you may be able to mix it up with floats and time on private water. There are services (or hosts such as I) that customize such weeks to suit their clients' needs and desires. Usually you stay in a centrally located hotel. The best fishing can be accessed in the surrounding area, and plans can be changed to accommodate weather and water conditions.

A lot of anglers travel on their own with only a guidebook in hand. But even excellent anglers can struggle without some sort of guidance. The guidebook will help, and these anglers might be able to read water and fish impeccably, but they don't know the variables that take years to learn: fish populations, access, timing. Then there are stretches of water that poachers are prevalent on—where trees and brush line a river and hide their doings. Even though all water is public in Argentina, that is theory only. And you have to be around for awhile before you learn which fields can be walked across.

When I was taking a lot of people fishing in Argentina, freelance anglers from the United States and abroad were common at the hotel I liked. Such experienced fly fishers might barely say hello when they arrived at the hotel, but after they realized how many more good fish we were catching, they'd friendly up pretty good, start eavesdropping, then introduce themselves and pump me for information. I'd have to get scarce because I couldn't give secrets away—that betrays the people we work with and for. When I was finally cornered, my standard reply was to suggest a guide. The best guides and water would be booked, but there would usually be some decent guides—and water—available.

Kingfisher under Lanin Volcano in Argentina.

New Zealand, Argentina, and Chile

New Zealand is known for its challenging—but excellent—fly fishing. And although the methods are often quite traditional, the game usually means sight fishing for very large brown trout. The regular cut of American fly fishers may be frustrated here. Having good casting skills, walking long distances, and paying the expense of helicopters might be required. Tasmania has good lake fishing for trout but not much for stream fishing.

Argentina is friendlier than New Zealand for the *average* fisherman. There are lots of wadable rivers and float fishing. The fishing style is familiar to most American fishers: dry flies, hopper/droppers, nymphs, and streamers. But there are the usual challenges of brush to cast under, wind to cast through, and long walks to undertake. Much of the fishing is easy to reach and close to airports at Junin and San Martin de Los Andes, Bariloche, and Esquel.

Fly fishing for trout is somewhat different in Chile than it is in Argentina. Generally there are more fish-eating locals in Chile, and hence greater effort is required to get to the best water. There are many remote and deep rivers in the south that need to be floated. The waters are generally harder to get to, and it rains *a lot* on that side of the Andes. Since the tragic earthquake hit the hub city of Santiago, there must be less access to the fishing, but less pressure on the water probably means good fishing.

People often confuse the huge sea-run browns of southern South America and Tierra del Fuego with the regular trout in northern Patagonia. These are totally different zones and are a thousand dusty miles apart. And it is impractical to fish both places in one trip. Separate flights would be required out of Buenos Aires. The sea-run brown fishing is very expensive, and the best of it is booked years in advance. But even if you reserve a choice spot, there will still be the famous wind to deal with, and many people refuse to return because of it.

Which brings up the fact that people commonly bite off more than they can chew on these trips. When too much is crammed into one holiday, the angler returns home exhausted and, likely, nearly skunked. When I started taking people fishing in Argentina, we would make plans to fish half the continent over a long weekend. After a period of years we found that, unless sufficient time is allowed, moving a lot was not that enjoyable or productive for the average fly fisher. Admittedly, these days my clients and I are of a mature disposition. The young and the restless are a different story and thrive on struggle and stress. A great compromise for all is a camp float. And although the planning and logistics are troublesome, in Argentina camping and floating provide the best access to unfished water.

CAMPING

Being fluid in your travel plans often means better—and cheaper—fishing. Don't be afraid to camp if the opportunity arises. No matter where you are, better fishing is a ways from a motel, and if you sleep by the water you are going to get lots more fishing in. But the problem can be that there is often nowhere to camp. Either camping is prohibited, or there is just nowhere to get off the road.

ATTITUDE

I've often found a self-defeating attitude in traveling anglers, many of whom have been spoiled by tailwaters and/or big stocked trout. Having invested money in the travel, they expect to find easy fishing waiting for them. If you are thinking "big fish in every pool," this attitude will negatively affect your planning. I remember chatting up a fly fisher from South Africa at an airport in Argentina. He thought that the fishing was going to be so spectacular that he "hadn't bothered with waders." A couple of days later he was searching for me at the hotel. When he found me hiding out in my room, I lent him some wading shoes and suggested a place he could fish.

It is all pretty much a crapshoot. Good trout fishing is where and when you find it—maybe just down the road or thousands of miles away. It's nice that it is spread out in such beautiful corners of the world.

PRIVATE WATER

Normally there are two types of private water: clubs where members can fish on their own and places that allow access only with a guide.

Many anglers balk at having to hire a guide, but landowners want clients escorted to protect the land and fish and to avoid the hassle of dealing with individuals and their complications. (I instruct my guides when dealing with busy ranchers to not make any waves—don't ask to bring along your girlfriend or pony.)

The cost of a day's catch-and-release on private water is usually a bargain at under $100. If your guide suggests that price, be aware that he is probably not making anything extra but simply wants a successful day. Also be aware that this is an environmentally sound contribution and that you are encouraging good care of the waters. The extra money might mean fewer cows or homes on the stream.

Most private waters, holding larger and smarter fish, are geared to more experienced fishermen, and the beginner will have a hard time getting the fly presented politely enough. And if the new fly fisher becomes hooked onto a larger fish, he or she may not know what to do with it.

Even on private water the quality of the fishing is contingent on how many rods have been on the water. When I call about booking a private section of river, I ask about the amount of pressure in the previous week.

If a lot of rods have been waving above a stretch of private water, we change our plans and fish public water instead. Many anglers who fish only private water may not realize that good fishing is almost always possible on public water—by driving and hiking farther. Sadly, the modern American is becoming more and more predisposed to pay rather than work or walk.

Book private water in advance because the space might be limited. We have a lonely property on the Brazos River here in New Mexico where, even though the cost is considerable, the fishing is so good that clients will often book a spot for the next year before they've even reached the locked gate on their way out.

You Should Have
Been Here Yesterday

If all of the little tricks in this book fail you, here is my final advice.

I'm a professional in the fly-fishing business. That means that, like every professional, I know what to do when things aren't going well: make up an excuse. I have spent considerable time exploring the evasive world of the fishing excuse, and not being able to repeat the same one, I have had to develop many.

THE TRIED-AND-TRUE EXCUSE

First, make the most use out of the tried-and-true "You should have been here yesterday." It is hard to beat because it proclaims, "Yes, there are fish in the river" and "You are close to having caught them." Be sure to find out if the inquirer had actually fished yesterday. If he or she had, then "You should have been here yesterday" obviously needs expansion to "You should have been here last week," or "month," or "year," depending on the date of his or her last outing.

BLAME IT ON MOTHER NATURE

When designing a proper excuse, remember to draw attention away from yourself. You can't say, "I can't fish very well, so I didn't catch any." No, you have to insert "because." It's because "the moon was full," or "there was no moon." "The water was too muddy," or it was "too clear." The water (or the air temperature) was "too warm" or "too cold." "The air was too windy" or "too still." "The weather was too rainy" or "too dry." You don't have to look far for an intelligent-sounding excuse. The whole natural world is waiting to be at fault, and best of all, it can't talk back.

WHEN THE WIND IS FROM THE WEST, THE FISHING IS THE BEST

You have to be careful, however, not to paint yourself into a corner. I learned that as a kid on one of my first guiding jobs. I had no idea how to catch fish in the lake at which we found ourselves, so I needed to point an accusing finger somewhere. You'd think I would have been safe finding fault with wind direction with four from which to choose. A convenient east wind made me look good at the start because everyone knows that "when the wind is out of the east, the fishing is the least." This worked for awhile, but it was a swirly sort of day. Still, thinking that the breeze would never do a 180, I unfortunately muttered, "When the wind is from the west, the fishing is the best." When the dreaded west wind arrived, I rowed in circles attempting to disorient the client.

THE ONE-WORD REPLY

At least other fishers have sympathy with bad luck because we've all been there. The person who doesn't fish is a tougher sell. I particularly dread encounters with rafters. These idlers already have an attitude against us because they don't know how to fish and just aimlessly float down the river. Between the brief moments of exhilaration that the rapids provide they search for a hapless angler to molest. They travel in loose packs, with boats spaced just far enough apart so that each group gets to ask, "How they bitin'?" The brief conversation is reiterated with each gang, and if you've caught some fish, you don't mind the question. You might even welcome it. If, however, you haven't had any success, answering in the negative over and over is ego deflating. If the water is running fast, they sail by mercifully quickly, but an elaborate excuse is then impossible, and you are reduced to a brief "yes" or "no" answer. What is needed here is some sort of stylish, one-word comeback. I heard one in the Caribbean a few years ago that has the proper attitude. While walking by an old Bahamian gentleman who was sleepily sitting over his "trow line," I gave him the old "Are they biting?" Without breaking his restful stride, he replied, "Presently."

The fly fisher, with his endless theories, tiny flies, and skinny leaders, has a bottomless pool of excuses. Fly fishing is an equal-opportunity sport in which the not-so-talented can make up for not catching by accumulating knowledge. This information may help catch a fish from time to time, but its real use is in the crafting of the clever fishing excuse. Failure can be turned into relative success by adopting a pensive air and saying, "I knew that they were taking No. 22 spent Tricos, so I went with a 7X tippet. But although I played the creature with impunity, it was just too fine a leader, and the bloody fish broke me off . . ."

CATCH-AND-RELEASE OPENS NEW OPPORTUNITIES

Catch-and-release fishing allows the unlucky angler even greater victories and puts us in a place where an excuse isn't even needed. That place lies just beyond a bend in the river, out of sight from your fishing partner. You are now free to say, "I knew that they were taking No. 22 spent Tricos and that I would have to go with a 7X tippet—I played the monster with impunity and released the brute unscathed."

Another tactic is to bypass or rise above mere fishing. Shift your priorities a little to accommodate the situation. For instance, a poor day on the water can handily be turned into a great picnic. "Fish? Yeah, I think we caught some. Hell, I forget. It was such a nice day in that beautiful place—and that lunch!" Or you can transcend such earthly pursuits and rise to a spiritual level higher than a dry-fly purist. Quote something from Jung, like "I ply the depths of my soul when I fish." Who's going to hassle you when you hand out that kind of jive?

I recently guided a North American businessman in Argentina who had one week to catch all the fish in Patagonia. On his last day he pounded the water like Rambo on a rampage in the face of one of the best fishing excuses known—a windy cold front. When he finally gave up he was too depressed for me to humor him with any of my flippant lines. He didn't say a word all the way back to town, and that gave me time to reflect on how important catch-and-release fly fishing really is.

While Rambo sulked, my line of thinking directed me to a new tactic. This season, when I get pestered about the quality of the fishing, I'm going to say, "Fishing! People are eating rocks and sticks, our country resembles ancient Rome before the fall, dogs are sleeping with cats, and lawyers openly high-five each other. The world is a crumbling, stumbling wreck, and you want to talk about a fish."

If you hear me say something like that, you can bet the fishing sucked, and, yes, "You should have been here yesterday."

Fish with Taylor Streit

Taylor Streit and his son Nick run Taos Fly Shop (and his guiding business Streit Fly Fishing) out of Taos, New Mexico. They fish the Rio Grande, Conejos, and Chama Rivers in both New Mexico and southern Colorado. His staff of guides teaches fly fishing and casting while on the water. Their intuitive style of instruction takes the mystery out of what may appear to be a complicated sport.

In the winter they take anglers to Patagonia, Argentina. These trips are customized to each group's needs and arranged so that the clients experience the unique Argentine lifestyle.

Streit conducts schools and clinics and speaks to fly-fishing clubs. He also conducts schools for guides based on *Instinctive Fly Fishing*. He can be reached at www.taosflyshop.com or by telephone at (575) 751-1312.

Steve Hicks

Index

About the Author

Taylor Streit has guided fly fishermen for thirty years—primarily in New Mexico but in the Bahamas and Argentina as well. In 2001 he was unanimously inducted into the Freshwater Fishing Hall of Fame as a legendary guide. The author of *Man vs Fish*, as well as a popular book on fly fishing New Mexico, he also writes for various magazines and newspapers. He lives in Taos, New Mexico, near his favorite river—the wild Rio Grande.